P9-EDC-654

# Reflections of a Scientist

# Reflections of a Scientist

Henry Eyring

Edited and with a Foreword
by
Harden Romney Eyring

Deseret Book Company
Salt Lake City, Utah

Parts of this book appeared in a slightly different form in Henry Eyring, *Faith of a Scientist* (Salt Lake City: Bookcraft, 1967); Edward L. Kimball, "A Dialogue with Henry Eyring," *Dialogue: A Journal of Mormon Thought* 8, no. 3/4 (autumn/winter 1974); and Steven Harvey Heath, "Henry Eyring, Mormon Scientist" (master's thesis, University of Utah, 1980.) I extend my thanks for permission to use this material.



First printing March 1983
First printing with revised pagination and typography, October 1998

Library of Congress Catalog Card Number 83-70109

ISBN 1-57345-409-5

Printed in the United States of America 10246-6385

10 9 8 7 6 5 4 3 2 1

# CONTENTS

# FOREWORD

Elder Neal A. Maxwell has said of his friend: "Though Henry Eyring is, in my opinion, the most distinguished Mormon scientist of this dispensation, Henry's highest expression of scholarship was seen in his capacity to grasp the simplest but most sublime truths about God, man, and the universe!"

In addition to his scholarship, Dad was a truly interesting character. Each summer for two decades following 1959 the Distinguished Professor of Chemistry at the University of Utah challenged all comers among his students to a fifty-yard dash. He gladly accepted challenges from other gladiators as well, but restrained himself from general challenges to the faculty and administration for fear that aspirants, even those half his age, might hurt themselves in the quest. He beat his secretary, to her surprise, and twice showed his dust to fellow administrators. However, with the field filled with able-bodied graduate students, he lost year after year, but he never came in last. "They only run if they think they can beat me. The nice, slow ones abstain," he would complain good naturedly. "I don't know how any intelligent person can continue to do this. I'd like to think I could win a prize. I'd just like to win anything."

Of course Dad knew very well what he was winning. He was winning friends for himself and for his university, community, church, and family—for all that mattered to him. He enjoyed being a character, but more because he thought it increased his influence for good than from any urge to be different.

A member of the National Academy of Sciences, he held fifteen honorary doctorates, both national and international, and some eighteen prizes, including the National Medal of Science, the Priestly Medal, the Berzelius Medal in Gold awarded by the Swedish Academy, and Israel's $100,000 Wolf Prize awarded in 1980. He was president of the two top scientific associations in his field, the American Chemical Society and the American Association for the Advancement of Science. He published more than six hundred papers and half a dozen books. Often, he listed the student coauthors' names first.

He would sometimes welcome distinguished visitors by challenging them to a standing floor-to-table-top jumping contest. This usually resulted in his demonstrating the feat and collecting the win by default, since not everyone was as able as he was to ignore the prospect of the painfully bruised shins that could result from the occasional miss.

Henry Eyring was born February 20, 1901, in Colonia Juarez, one of the Latter-day Saint colonies in Mexico. He was the first son and third child of Edward and Caroline Romney Eyring. Camilla Eyring Kimball, wife of President Spencer W. Kimball, is Dad's older sister. He joked that being born in 1901 put his age just one year behind the century date and that he'd been running hard all his life to catch up.

His early years riding with his father over their large and prosperous ranch were always vividly enjoyed in his memory and stories.

He was always a good student, although his love for fun may have sometimes tried his teachers and associates. He recalled, "It was in the third grade that Ola Martineau sat in front of my friend Viv Bentley and me. Ola had the interesting habit of sucking her thumb, which we thought was a little bit juvenile, and we felt we ought to do all we could to help her overcome it. We had no better way of impressing her problem on her than to put her very lovely blonde curls in an inkwell whenever she'd suck her thumb. Now, we didn't do it otherwise, since we were only trying to help her. There was no idea of pleasure for us, of course. Why her mother didn't whip us I have no idea, but I guess she was glad we weren't any worse."

The Mexican revolution in 1912 brought an abrupt change in circumstances. The Mormon colonists had to leave Mexico, and the Eyring family finally settled in Pima, Arizona. Here Dad, in addition to enjoying his teenage years, learned to work hard and developed his compulsion for giving more than he received or was expected of him.

He won a scholarship to the University of Arizona, where he studied mining engineering and metallurgy, then went on for his Ph.D. in chemistry at the University of California at Berkeley.

He was teaching at the University of Wisconsin when he met Mildred Bennion at a Christmas party. They were later married and raised three sons: Edward M., professor of Chemistry at the University of Utah, Henry B., member of the Quorum of the Twelve Apostles, and myself, Harden R., executive assistant to the commissioner of the Utah System of Higher Education.

In 1946, after fifteen distinguished years at Princeton University, Mom prevailed upon Dad to move "home" to Utah, where he became dean of the graduate school at the University of Utah and was influential in developing a first-rate university there. Dad was always delighted with the move to Utah. He enjoyed being close to his many relatives and, particularly with the advent of jet travel, he felt just as able to keep up with his many professional interests around the country and the world from Salt Lake City as from New Jersey. He continued to work full-time at his teaching and research, in a building named after him, into his eighty-first year, garnishing honors all along the way.

Dad died December 26, 1981. At that time we had been working on this book for five years and talking about it for more. It is a summary of his ideas, expressed in countless talks and articles, about the faith of a scientist. The ideas have been a part of me from my earliest recollections. I have spent hundreds of hours over the last forty years talking to Dad about Mexico, Pima, Princeton, and science and religion. This is my family liturgy and heritage. The ideas seem so obvious and true to me that I am always surprised when I find someone who thinks otherwise and won't yield to a persuasive recitation of my father's wisdom. Of course, one of Dad's fundamental tenets was that being tolerant and having respect for a diversity of ideas is the happiest way to sift and winnow for the truth. Just keep pecking away until you find it, and allow others to do the same.

People who knew Dad through his public speaking would often remark that it must be fun living with such a "laugh-a-minute" character. Actually, Dad loved and worked at his chemistry almost all his waking hours and often in the middle of the night, if he happened to wake up. Sometimes he would be sitting in church, looking very attentive, and would then pull out an envelope and start writing some new mathematical equation. The speaker never knew that the mesmerized look on Dad's face was for the chemistry going through his head and not the sermon being delivered from the pulpit.

At home, in the evenings, he didn't want a private study. He liked to sit in the living room, even with the radio going and his family playing, reading, and discussing around him. He had the ability to "tune out" and do his chemistry but still be a part of the goings-on.

He was proud of his family. He gave Mom the credit for raising my brothers and me, while he roamed the valleys and passes of chemical kinetics and other scientific sites of his imagination. Certainly Mildred Bennion was a remarkable woman, and whatever her sons amount to has a good deal to do with her. But Dad, too, had his impact, and for me the contents of this book reflect the force of his personality and presence.

Also, his discipline was gentle, but effective. I hated to displease him. He would look so annoyed and grumpy. But when I did something really dumb, he would commiserate with me and tell a story on himself. For example, as a thirteen-year-old, I took our new 1951 Ford sedan joyriding. Even with a pillow under me, I could barely touch the pedals and see out the windshield at the same time. Approaching the driveway on my return, I panicked as a car pulled up behind me. I went too fast and hit our house. Fortunately, it was made of brick, or I would have parked the car in the living room. The shrubs didn't need trimming for years.

Mom tolerated me and made me pay the full damages to the car from my paper-route money over the next year. My brothers ostracized me from their company and conversations. But Dad told me a story. He related how he had taken his father's gun down from over the fireplace and had gone out onto the front porch to frighten a neighbor boy going past the house. Thinking the gun to be unloaded, he had aimed it and pulled the trigger. It went off with a roar. "Fortunately," he said, "I was a terrible shot, and missed him." From his face and voice, I knew that the fear and horror of an event that might have changed his life still plagued him. Thus, his story eased my embarrassment and misery. No matter how busy he was, I always knew I was the apple of his eye. He loves me. And I love him.

Dad accomplished many things and received many honors in the world. However, I think his "finest hour" is probably known only to his family and a very few others. This was his devotion and selflessness during our mother's long illness. He knew that he had health problems of his own but refused to consider taking the time out to look after them. He cooked food, washed dishes, kept house, cancelled appointments and meetings all over the world, and spent time with his wife. He became an expert on cancer and sought to contribute to the body of knowledge that might save her life. Finally, as the end neared and she was hospitalized in painful, drugged unconsciousness, he slept the last ten days on a cot in her hospital room in case she might need something. When Mom died in 1969, he had only one desire: that as she passed to the other side she would not be alone, but that her family and friends would be there to meet her.

Dad then proceeded with the medical tests that confirmed his own cancer of the prostate. He went to Stanford for medical treatment and then again took up his busy scientific schedule. It was a hard, lonely time.

Two years later Dad met and married Winifred Brennan, which added four new sisters to our family: Eleanor, Pat, Joan, and Bernice. The next ten years were good and full, but the last few months of 1981 became hard and uncomfortable.

In the final months and weeks of Dad's life, he experienced the focusing power of a great and awful illness. Finally, in the last few days, all pretense was stripped away. Only the truth remained. He saw his family and friends clearly, including those things we could improve upon. He gave up the companionship of his beloved molecules only at the very last. Within days of his death, he was still working on a scientific book with a colleague. But finally the pain was too great to enjoy escape even into that world of chemistry that had filled his life so fully for so long.

There remained only two things. The first was complete love and admiration for his father, Edward Christian Eyring. The boyhood days of riding the range with "Papa" and learning how to live life well and fully remained completely vivid and precious. The second was a never-wavering certainty that a better life awaited him. He spoke with anticipation and longing of the release from pain and the reunion with those he loved who had preceded him to the other side.

The nights brought no rest or sleep. I have the vivid recollection of one such night when I returned to the bedroom to find Dad on his knees beside his bed, beseeching his Heavenly Father for strength and help. My brother Hal recalls a night spent in a conversation about Grandpa and the better life to come. Winifred tells of one occasion when he asked rhetorically, "Why is God doing this to me?" He then fell asleep, and when he awoke several hours later, he remarked in answer to his own question, "God needs men of courage. He is testing my courage."

Henry Eyring was a prominent reference point in our lives. He was fixed and certain. He used his self-deprecating humor to teach us how to live. He never told jokes on others, only on himself. I know God loves him, as all who know him do, and that He has taken him to a good place, with friends and family and interesting chemistry. I suspect he has already challenged the whole place to a footrace.

The apostles of old and Joseph Smith sealed their testimonies with their blood. Henry Eyring sealed his testimony on the rack of bone cancer. That rack stripped away all artifice. He was true and faithful to his testimony of the gospel to the very last. This book contains the truth as understood by Henry Eyring. I hope it will help those of us who must now journey without him.

HARDEN R. EYRING

# ACKNOWLEDGMENTS

I express appreciation to my wife and children for helping me hibernate in the study for months on end; to Winifred Eyring for collecting tapes and articles, hither and yon; to Edward Kimball for particularly rich grist for the mill; to my brothers for suggestions, encouragement, and help in proofreading; and most of all, to Henry Eyring, a good father as well as a great and happy man.

# INTRODUCTION

Virtually everything in this book has probably been part of a talk I gave somewhere, sometime. I really have only one talk. My first wife, Mildred, used to think I should prepare something different each time I spoke. I told her that I'd been preparing for forty years and that any last-minute cramming wasn't going to help much. My second wife, Winifred, is very nice; she acts as though she's never heard my talks before. But, if you think it's hard on her to sit there and listen, just think about me. I've heard it all more times than anyone else. The only merciful thing is that I forget what I've said and written before, so my talks get a little different each time.

World leaders like the President of the Church face a different situation. Everything they say is published. Mercifully, no one ever publishes anything I say, and nobody ever comes back a second time to hear me speak, so I can use the same talk over and over. There are advantages to being a poor speaker.

When I talk in church, I am really talking to myself. I always have a ready subject. I just pick out one of my faults to preach about, and that takes care of about as many talks as I need to give.

I'm also a firm believer in Mary Poppins's prescription: "A spoonful of sugar helps the medicine go down." I can remember getting castor oil and cod liver oil as a child. Just one sneeze or wheeze and out came the medicine. This was a great incentive for me to stay healthy. (I've suspected shock treatments of having the same value. You'd have to be really crazy not to get better after the first one, in order to avoid the second.) Well, in teaching the gospel, some gentle good humor seems to help the true principles stick in the heart and mind. My foibles are so naturally comical that I don't seem to have any trouble in this regard.

I am a visual thinker, both in my science and in my religious life. When I pray, I "see" God in my mind's eye. It helps me get down to specifics if I'm speaking to him face to face. It's not a detailed impression—I couldn't tell you whether we are indoors or out. I really notice only his eyes. They are looking at me, and he is smiling. When you think how big the universe is and how many more interesting things must be happening than anything I could possibly have to say, you must admit it's nice to have the feeling that you have God's full and complete attention, whenever you pray. He doesn't have to speak. Somehow my meandering thoughts seem to arrive at a better solution than I had come up with until then.

When I think about absolute reaction rate theory, I first get in my mind the image of a potential energy surface that is like a mountain pass between two valleys. I then can count the number of molecules in the first valley, or energy state, that are eligible candidates to participate in the reaction. They have to get excited to get up to the top of the pass, where they are also further apart. About half of them bump together hard enough to exchange partners and form the new molecules that then quiet down into the next valley at a lower energy state. After I have put the picture together, I am ready to do the necessary mathematics to describe what I have seen, which will then predict the results that will come from experimental verifications.

It helps to have a model of what is happening before trying to quantify a problem. A good model is best, but a bad model is better than nothing. Generally, a good model is simple. It's less of a sin to be simple and wrong than to be complicated and wrong. To develop a suitable model, I ask myself, "How would I act if I were an atom or a molecule and found myself in this situation?"

Rates of cooking, or growth of muscles, or tightening of muscles, or using the brain—everything involves the speed of some reaction. Understanding these reactions really means getting acquainted with the molecules as if they were your friends and knowing what their nature is and what they will do, how hard you have to throw them at one another so they will change partners. It is like a detective story, and every time you get a nice new tool, you can solve some puzzles.

The sense of smell is an interesting example. Before you set off describing it with mathematics, it helps to understand that when your nose picks up a strong odor, such as gasoline, frying bacon, or chopped onions, it is really smelling the shape of molecules floating through the air. The nose can distinguish some fifteen thousand different compounds. It is a pianolike machine with the nerve endings similar to the keys and a molecule like a player. Each molecule plays a different tune on your nose.

In teaching science, it is important to help the student "see" things like the random behavior of molecules, how they "forget" where they are going and start off in a new direction and generally stagger around like drunks at a New Year's party. I've never been drunk myself, but I can imagine how it would be and can do a pretty good job of imitating it in order to get the point across.

Perhaps the greatest gift a teacher can give to a student is the sense of complete enjoyment that comes from immersion in the subject being taught. Chemistry is fun. So is scripture study, or world history, or economics, or any other subject, once you get into it and see and feel it all over.

I have found that in an effort to understand the world around us and my place in it, there is a fascination that never ceases to enthrall me, and I wonder if this is not the secret of happiness. Stated differently, each of us should find a worthy cause big enough that we can usefully and happily dedicate our lives to it and then follow wherever it leads. And we can teach others to do the same.

To help myself do this, I try to follow three basic axioms or postulates that have largely guided my entire life. They are:

1. God is a kind, loving, benevolent Father who likes me, and all his children, and will patiently work with us to help us be as good as we can be. You might ask, "What about his washing the world clean of the wicked with the great flood at the time of Noah? Or his burning the wicked as stubble next time?" These don't seem completely patient and forgiving. But I see the flood as proving my point precisely, if we view it from an eternal perspective. According to scripture (1 Peter 3:18–20), those drowned in the flood were the very first people Christ went to see after his death, even before he was resurrected and ascended to his Father. He hadn't given up on even the wicked he had washed off the earth. So, God the Father and his Son, Jesus Christ, like me, and they like you too.

2. God is so enormously wise that to him my feeble efforts must seem childlike at best. I just work here. So, although God likes me, I think it is more for my potential than for anything I have done or am likely to do in this life. This axiom helps me keep myself (and all the rest of you) in perspective. We all make mistakes. That's nothing to be particularly ashamed of or excited about. We should just keep plugging away.

3. We should put more into everything we do than we take out. Even if I operate a business for profit, I should be sure the customers are getting a full measure. Also, the key to personal freedom is to be putting so much in voluntarily that no one ever has to remind us of the rules and regulations for minimum behavior. Heavenly Father and Jesus

Christ are perfect examples of putting more in than they take out. We are forever in their debt.

The application of these axioms in one's life can result in some pretty interesting behavior. I don't know whether I am proud, maybe even a little bit arrogant, because God loves me, or humble because I can so readily admit my mistakes. And so on. In any case, the chapters that follow illustrate some of the results of these axioms.

# TRUTH

All day long, on a fiercely hot Friday in September 1919, I hauled hay in Pima, Arizona. On Monday I was going to start classes at the University of Arizona, where I was to study mining engineering. In the evening my father, as fathers often do, felt that he'd like to have a last talk with his son. He wanted to be sure I'd stay on the straight and narrow. He said, "Henry, won't you come and sit down. I want to talk to you."

Well, I'd rather do that than pitch hay any time. So, I went over and sat down with him.

"We're pretty good friends, aren't we?"

"Yes," I said, "I think we are."

"Henry, we've ridden together on the range, and we've farmed together. I think we understand each other. Well, I want to say this to you: I'm convinced that the Lord used the Prophet Joseph Smith to restore His Church. For me, that is a reality. I haven't any doubt about it. Now, there are a lot of other matters that are much less clear to me. But in this Church you don't have to believe anything that isn't true. You go over to the University of Arizona and learn everything you can, and whatever is true is a part of the gospel. The Lord is actually running this universe. And I want to tell you something else: if you go to the University and are not profane, if you'll live in such a way that you'll feel comfortable in the company of good people, and if you go to church and do the other things that we've always done, I won't worry about your getting away from the Lord."

That's about the best advice I ever got. It has simplified my life. All I have to do is live in a wholesome way, which is best for me anyway, and be busy about finding truth wherever I can. I suspect that you would enjoy that formula too.

The significant thing about a scientist is this: he simply expects the truth to prevail because it *is* the truth. He doesn't work very much on the reactions of the heart. In science, the thing *is*, and its being so is something one cannot resent. If a thing is wrong, nothing can save it, and if it is right, it cannot help succeeding.

So it is with the gospel. I once had the privilege of attending a youth conference and responding to questions of the assembled young people. A young man asked, "In high school we are taught such things as pre-Adamic men, but we hear another thing in Church. What should I do about it?"

I think I gave the right answer. I said, "In this Church, you only have to believe the truth. Find out what the truth is!"

This Church is not worried about that question or other similar questions, because the Church is committed only to the truth. I do not mean to say that individuals in the Church always know the whole truth, but we have the humility sometimes to say we do not know all the answers about these things.

Some have asked me, "Is there any conflict between science and religion?" There is no conflict in the mind of God, but often there is conflict in the minds of men. Through the eternities, we are going to get closer and closer to understanding the mind of God; then the conflicts will disappear.

I'm happy to represent a people who, throughout their history, have encouraged learning and scholarship in all fields of honorable endeavor, a people who have among their scriptural teachings such lofty concepts as these: "The glory of God is intelligence, or, in other words, light and truth." (D&C 93:36.) "It is impossible for a man to be saved in ignorance." (D&C 131:6.) "Whatever principle of intelligence we attain unto in this life, it will rise with us in the resurrection." (D&C 130:18.)

To us has come the following, which we regard as a divine injunction: "Teach ye diligently and my grace shall attend you, that you may be instructed more perfectly in theory, in principle, in doctrine, in the law of the gospel, in all things that pertain unto the kingdom of God, that are expedient for you to understand; of things both in heaven and in the earth, and under the earth; things which have been, things which are, things which must shortly come to pass; things which are at home, things which are abroad; the wars and the perplexities of the nations, and the judgments which are on the land; and a knowledge also of countries and of kingdoms." (D&C 88:78–79.)

Here is the spirit of true religion, an honest seeking after knowledge of all things of heaven and earth.

# HEREDITY AND ENVIRONMENT

Once, after World War II, I was teasing a Belgian a little bit. He said, "There has never been a good German, ever!" I said, "There must have been one by *mistake* sometime." He then asked me what nationalities I came from, and I replied, "I'm half German and half English." He said, "The worst two nations on earth!" Apparently, considering my hereditary background, you may want to take serious thought before continuing with this book.

It takes several ingredients to make a good scientist. One is being bright, in seeing and grasping ideas quickly. Another is a sense of self-worth that allows you to keep struggling along even when you might seem lost in the woods for the moment. It seems to me that both heredity and environment play a role in these attributes. Undoubtedly, the prospective scientist should arrange to be born with the right genes. Anyone who has examined the differences between individuals with presumably equal training cannot escape this conclusion. However, even a gifted person requires a stimulating environment.

Ideally, a stimulating environment also provides a sense of safety and well-being. It might even make you feel a little better about yourself than a completely unbiased evaluation would seem to warrant. Lowell Bennion, speaking from his wide experience in teaching in the LDS Institute at the University of Utah, said it this way: "At first I thought the big problem of university students would be questions in logic and philosophy, but I soon found out that when they were happy and socially accepted, their imagined difficulties melted away."

To illustrate this with my own life, let me tell you about a happy childhood that may seem long ago and far away to you, but seems yesterday and close to me.

I was born in 1901 and grew up on ranches and farms in Mexico and Arizona in a devoutly Mormon family. I don't remember my grandfather Henry Eyring, since he died the year after I was born. I grew up with the image (from what my parents had told me) of him giving me a name and a blessing when I was a baby. They said he was so pleased with his namesake that he cried. Likewise, I am delighted to bear his name.

Grandfather, who spoke seven languages and was well educated in his native Germany, came to America as an eighteen-year-old with his sister, after his father had lost the family fortune in a business venture. Grandfather said later that the loss was actually a blessing because he was more susceptible to the teachings of the Church as a clerk in a wholesale drug firm in St. Louis than he would have been as a prosperous apothecary in Germany.

In later life he ran a cooperative store in Colonia Juarez, one of the Mormon colonies in Mexico. It was said that he could have run it as his own business, for his own profit, but chose to continue as a cooperative because that benefited others. Porfirio Díaz, president of the Mexican republic for thirty years, stated in a letter that Henry Eyring was one of the most strictly honest men he had ever met. Such a grandfather, especially one with the same name, was and is a great comfort and strength to me.

I remember visiting Grandmother Eyring. Her maiden name was Mary Bommeli. She was from Canton Turgau in

Switzerland, where she and other family members had joined the Church. She helped send her family to Utah and stayed behind to earn her own passage. She and Henry Eyring met as fellow pioneers in an 1860 wagon train west. Grandfather described the trip as follows: "On my journey across the plains I became acquainted with [Mary] . . . , and we had many pleasant and useful conversations with each other while walking to-gether in advance of the train. . . . I enjoyed myself excellently while crossing the plains, walking nearly the whole distance, and to me it was more like a pleasure trip, than a toilsome pilgrimage."

Grandmother was stake Relief Society president in Mexico well into her eighties. She would drive two hundred miles or more in her buggy to visit all the Relief Society organizations in the stake.

I would go often to see my Grandmother Eyring. She lived in a paradise, as far as she could make it. There were roses and flowers everywhere, and lots of grapes. She was always working in her garden—hauling manure in a wheelbarrow from the corral, putting it over her sandy soil, then watering it enough so that the garden was always beautiful. Nothing else in town was as nice, I don't think.

The first thing she'd do whenever she'd see me coming was to go down to the cellar and bring me two big, red apples. She was too busy with her own thoughts to spend much time hearing any of my wisdom. She had more interesting things to do, but she was awfully nice to me.

The Piedras Verde River ran along the west side of our property in the town of Colonia Juarez. Our ranch was about seven miles outside of town. When I was two years old, I was put up on my father's unsaddled horse while my mother and father led the horse to the river for a drink after a full day's work on the ranch. When the horse finished drinking, he shook himself, as horses do, and I fell into the river. As my father fished me out, I immediately asked to be put back on the horse. I never remember a time when I did not ride horses.

When I was four I had typhoid fever and nearly died. Two things came out of that incident that have made a lasting impression on me. The first was a visit from my Sunday School teacher. Miss Allred was an attractive young lady, and I was proud and happy that she cared enough to visit me. She spoke to me cheerfully and, after a brief visit with my mother and me, went her way. But something important had happened to me. I had been a vital part of a fine teacher-student relationship that I have never forgotten. I learned that day how important it is to care about people, even when they are small and may not seem very important.

The second event connected with my illness was the purchase by my father of two young goats to occupy my time as I recovered. I loved my goats, but they grew rapidly, and by the time I was better, they had discovered how to get into the neighbor's garden despite what appeared to be an adequate fence. They soon became a serious nuisance. My father's solution to the problem was not just to get rid of the goats, as most people would have done. One day he rode up to where I was playing, leading a young sorrel horse, and asked me if I would be willing to trade my two goats for the horse. I was delighted to make the trade, but named my new horse *Chivo*, which in Spanish means *goat*. What a wonderful thing, to give his four-year-old the extraordinary respect of bargaining with him as an equal. (Actually, Father was an excellent horse trader, so he gave me a considerably better bargain than a true equal would have enjoyed from him.)

My mother also bestowed constant and lavish praise on me and my brothers and sisters. From my earliest memories, Mother suffused the whole world with warmth and happiness. She was a strong, buoyant, wonderful person whom I took completely for granted.

To her the world and everything in it was beautiful and wonderful, and one couldn't help being swept along with her on a cloud of rosy optimism. Mother expected me to stand at the head of my class in school, and it never occurred to me to try for anything less. Very little was said about this directly, except that every small success was duly noted and appreciated. Mother and Father seldom scolded us, but never passed up a chance to commend us.

Mother was an inveterate worker. She never could rest. One of the things she did was to make woolen socks for me to wear in the winter. I think those socks were made from the kind of hair they used to make hair shirts to punish people with. The things would just stick into my legs like nothing else you ever saw, and I just hated those socks. I can remember one time trying to ease the pain by getting a bucket of water, pulling my sock out, and pouring water down it. This didn't seem to do much good. I was just as bad off after I wet them as I was before. Anyway, it was one of my early experiments. The happiest thing about spring was that we could take off our shoes and go barefoot. I liked that. In the summertime I always went barefoot.

In Mexico, my father was well-to-do and had accumulated a ten-thousand-acre fenced ranch for six hundred head of short-horn Durham cattle and a four-thousand-acre pasture and farmland where he kept from fifty to one hundred head of horses. On one occasion, when I was nine years old, the river through our ranch was at flood stage, and in order to get home, Father and I had to cross the dangerous river or go a long way out of our way to cross a bridge. I thought the river looked very risky, as trees were floating down it. If they were to hit our horses, it would be something of a nuisance. But Father said we could cross, and so we proceeded. He found a place where the river was running deep but slower, and then said, "You ride on the upstream side of me so I'll have a chance to grab you as you go by if your horse slips." We rode our horses across without incident, but I still remember with pleasure my father's confidence in me and my trust and confidence in him.

My father had a way of making everyone feel important. He was never patronizing and always treated people as individuals with rights that he respected. The result was that I would have tried to jump over the moon if I had thought he wanted me to do it.

It was fun to grow up with my father. Riding and working side by side with him everyday was one of the nice things that I had, that my sons haven't had, because we live in a different way. I liked that, except on those days when one of my cousins was having a birthday party and Father would still want me to go to the ranch with him. With over two hundred first cousins I missed a lot of parties.

I have a lot of fine brothers and sisters who I think are proof that there was something good about the combination of heredity and environment in that household, in spite of what you might think of me.

# THE CHURCH

While living in Mexico, I often saw vivid proof of the importance of the Church as an institution. It was the center of everything. In the Church, we weren't allowed to round dance, but I wasn't old enough to care. But we could square dance. We were just a little bit behind the times.

Then the Mexican Revolution came to disrupt our happy lives. I remember riding with Father and meeting about two hundred soldiers under Don José de la Luce Blanco. That means "Sir Joseph of the White Light." He was blue-eyed, with red whiskers—a Spaniard, of course. Often three or four Americans, soldiers of fortune, would be riding with the revolutionaries. I remember being quite disturbed when I saw this general, riding at the head of his troops, coming toward us on the road halfway between our two ranches, that is, the one that was about a mile from town and the one that was seven miles. I wondered if we shouldn't turn back. But Father laughed, and we rode up and talked to General Don José de la Luce Blanco, and he was friendly. Father told him something about directions and which way he could go, and so on, and then we went on up to the ranch. Father got on very well with the Mexican people. He spoke the language like a native. He liked people and they liked him.

However, more than once my father was coerced into supplying beef for revolutionaries in return for receipts that would be made good if the revolution were successful. There were also numerous exchanges of poor horses for well-bred Eyring horses.

One day a Mexican rebel by the name of Toribio Lara, who had been convicted of theft against the people of Juarez on at least three occasions and had each time been released without punishment, came intoxicated from Casa Grande. He attempted to break in the door of my Grandmother Eyring's home. He threatened to kill her unless she gave him $100, a gun, and ammunition. Only the intervention of neighbors prevented a tragedy.

On another occasion, I remember hearing the shot on a warm July day in 1912 when a Mexican, Juan Sosa, was killed in Juarez. Sosa had been accused of a number of thefts, and his arrest was ordered by the acting presidente of Colonia Juarez, Charles E. McClellan. A committee of men were asked to aid the city marshal in arresting Sosa, but as one of the men was climbing through a barbed wire fence, Sosa hit him with the end of his shovel, causing a serious wound. In defense, shots were fired at Sosa by several members of the posse. When it was over, Sosa lay dead on the ground. It took several days of intense negotiation before Mexican officials released members of the posse who had been transported to Casa Grande for a hearing before rebel general José Inez Salazar.

In late July 1912, General Salazar told Mormon leaders that no more assurances or guarantees could be extended, and, in fact, demanded the guns of the colonists to aid the revolutionary forces. The colonists gathered old guns and ammunition and turned them over to Salazar's men. In anticipation of this kind of trouble, the Mormons had earlier secured several shipments of new Springfield rifles and ammunition and had stored them in the bishop's storehouse in Juarez. The revolutionaries didn't know the new rifles were there and would have considered them extremely valuable. Had they realized the deception, they would have been furious.

The townspeople needed to keep them from finding out. My father told me how he, Miles A. Romney, and others smuggled the guns out the back door of the storehouse with Mexican forces encamped in front and the main street patrolled. The guns were taken to caves nearby and eventually to a place called "the stairs" near our ranch. The whole undertaking was extremely dangerous, and had it been discovered, it seems certain that bloodshed could not have been prevented.

The Church leaders met and decided to evacuate the women and children to El Paso. The men would remain behind to protect their property; then when things settled down, they would bring all of their families back. Almost before the exodus was finished, the Mexican rebels began looting the Mormon colonies. The men who had remained could see that their presence would not stop the looting, so it was fight or leave. Within the next ten days the Mormon men were together and on their way to El Paso.

In all, nearly five thousand of the Mormon people were forced to leave behind everything they could not carry and to seek refuge in El Paso. So what I saw was the Church, where law had disappeared, with its organization of stake presidents and bishops, bring us out of Mexico in as orderly a fashion as anything you can imagine. It was done perfectly. Everyone looked to his bishop, and the bishops looked to the stake and its high council. And I thought then, as I think now, that this is the Lord's church and that he is interested in every aspect of our lives. This gospel is functional, it really works. It's the proof that the Savior spoke of when he said to try it and see if it works. (See John 7:17.)

As a youngster I got a picture of this great church in action. I was born in the Church and was taught its principles since infancy, but I saw it work, and I have never forgotten it.

The only error made in the exodus was shipping me out with the women and children. After all, I was eleven years old and thought I should have remained with the men. Well, one mistake is not too bad.

# CHURCH LEADERS

I've known President Spencer W. Kimball for over sixty-five years. I've never seen or heard anything about him that didn't increase my admiration for him. Not everyone can say that about his brother-in-law. The Lord didn't make a mistake. Not that the Lord needs my endorsement. I don't think we've ever had a leader (and they've all been tremendous) with less ego to be administered to and who identifies himself more with everyone and likes everyone as well as Spencer W. Kimball does. Saying that is not self-serving, because I don't think he cares particularly what I think. But he likes me; at least I think so. That's a measure of how broadminded he is.

Just a thought about Camilla Kimball, my sister. I don't know anything she ever did that wasn't loving, except for the time she tried to put me into a dark closet. That's the only time I can remember her trying to correct me. I wasn't a bad boy, of course; I'm sure she just misunderstood me. She is six years older than I am, and just as she was about to push me into the dark closet and shut the door (I was struggling with everything I had and was filled with all the terror a small boy could have of being in that dark closet under the stairs) I called out, "You fool!" Camilla was devastated. She knew the scripture that says that a man who calls his brother a fool is in danger of hellfire. She was certain I was lost, and let me loose. I've struggled all my life to understand just how bad what I said was, but I still feel relieved that I didn't have to go into that closet. I'm sorry for what I said, and maybe that is repentance.

When I was nine years old and we were living in Mexico, my father was on the high council. High council meetings were held on Saturday, and a time or two Father forgot about his meeting until we had ridden most of the seven miles from our home in town to the ranch to do some chores. My father would say, "Oh my, it's high council today. I'll have to turn around and go back. You go ahead and see about the cattle we were talking about." I thought high council must be a pretty bad thing when it took him away and left me to do the work. But it isn't, it's a good thing. Of course, wives have that feeling also. They wonder why their husbands sit on the stand when they could be down in the congregation doing something useful like refereeing the children's squabbles.

Now *I'm* on the high council, and what I've noticed is that people of ability leave the high council to become bishops and mission presidents and other things, but if there isn't anything else you can do and you're not bad enough to be released, you just become more and more senior on the high council. So I'm now the senior high councilor in the Bonneville Stake. I think the president will want to keep me there since it's inconspicuous and I do very little harm.

I've had some wonderful opportunities to serve and observe the Brethren at work. I was put on the general board of the Sunday School before I even reached Salt Lake City in 1946. I was at a Sunday School convention in Idaho soon thereafter, and one of the good local brethren questioned me at some length about my family connections. Finally, I happened to mention that Adam S. Bennion, then a member of the Quorum of the Twelve, was my wife's cousin. "Ah ha!" he said. "That's why you're on the general board." Obviously, the quality of my presentations at the convention must have left him puzzled until he found my connection. I didn't have the heart to tell him about Spencer being my brother-in-law and Marion G. Romney being my cousin. Apparently, people are less perceptive in Salt Lake City than in Idaho, because it was twenty-five years before they realized I wasn't going to make a contribution and released me from the Sunday School board.

My day-to-day membership in various "best wards in the Church" have afforded me opportunity to observe our lay leadership. I have never seen a bishop I didn't admire. Maybe it's that I'm not very close in my observations. People have said of me that I think about the molecules to the point that I am confused. But I believe that you could not find a body of men anywhere in the world who are as high in their responsibility and their intention of doing good as the bishops of the Church. I know their salary. I served as a "small bishop," a branch president, in Princeton, New Jersey, for twelve years. Do you know what the salary was? Between about a minus 13 and 15 percent and half my time. When that kind of people preside over you, you can bet your life they believe in what they are doing. They either believe or they are kind of dumb to spend half their time and have their wives (not the good ones, of course) think they have gone off the deep end.

I've watched carefully what happens to that tithing that bishops and the rest of us pay. I've never seen any of it taken up into heaven. It is always used right here to help the people who are around us and to do the things that if we were thoughtful enough we would want to do ourselves. I'm convinced that the money I pay for tithing does more good than I do with the rest of it. I've never seen it misused.

The Church provides me with opportunities to work with other people. My home teaching families know quite accurately when I'm coming. I always get there by the end of the month, and generally there aren't too many guesses left. One can teach by a poor example as well as a good one, and I think I'm rather gifted in that respect.

Don't you enjoy the home teachers? I do. I've always had excellent home teachers. I believe the bishop has felt that I needed to be watched, and I appreciate having two wonderful people come to visit. We sometimes talk about history a little more than my wife thinks is necessary. She'd like to have just the meat of the gospel. I like that too, but I also like to hear about how things looked a long time ago to other brethren who are so prominent in our history.

I never miss a sacrament meeting. Sometimes, because of high council assignments and my own ward schedule, I attend more than one on a Sunday. I always get something useful out of them. Sometimes the talks being given from the pulpit are rather weak. Then I may have to listen awhile before I can figure out what the topic is, but once I have that, I start preparing in my mind a talk on the same subject. "What would I say if that were my theme?" I ask myself. Of course, I'd get more new ideas if I listened to the other fellow, but I enjoy my own thoughts, and I really do listen a lot of the time.

I believe in following counsel. I'd like to do all the things that the Brethren ask me to do. I'm convinced that the prophets are inspired and that I'll be inspired in guiding my family if I listen to them. When I don't follow the counsel of those who are placed over me, then I'm in very deep water. I'm enough of a coward and a poor enough swimmer that that's not where I want to be.

Still, I also like to see one of the Brethren make what appears to be a mistake now and then. I make them all the time. So, I think that if the Lord can use one of the Brethren and they're not perfect, then maybe he can find a way to use me. Some people get all worked up when someone important says something a little differently than they would say it. But I'm delighted. If I can see something less than perfection in our leaders, it gives me hope. I want to go to the celestial kingdom.

I sometimes fall asleep in the temple, but mostly I stay awake. I also doze in church occasionally, but that's because I trust my leaders. If I were worried about what they were doing, I'd stay wide awake.

# NOSE TO THE GRINDSTONE

You have to be more than bright to be a good scientist. You also have to be interested in what you do. You need to get lost among your friends, the molecules, and rather be roaming around with them than doing almost anything else. If science or whatever else you have chosen to do is just an eight-hour day and then on to other things, you're probably not going to change the world.

I have many of my best ideas at night. I come to work each morning with new ideas. Most of them are wrong, and it is the responsibility of my graduate students to help find the logical errors or the reasons why the ideas are not workable. After examination, about 5 to 10 percent of the ideas are inherently interesting and provide some insight into certain phenomena. Each day is a winnowing and sifting of ideas. You have to develop the ability to distinguish blind alleys from the right track.

It helps not to be too self-critical. Some people are perfectionists and can't stand the messy way most good ideas start. It's better to be a happy muddler.

After you suffer through elementary school, high school, and college, then you get paid well for having fun—it's ridiculous! Still, scientific research isn't all fun. I've written over six hundred scientific publications and an awful lot of proposals for funding, and yet I think of writing as a necessary part of the job, but no great sport. Huxley said, "Perhaps the most valuable result of all education is the ability to make yourself do the thing you have to do when it is to be done, whether you like it or not." I'm not sure educated people have the corner on the stick-to-it-iveness market, but wherever persistence comes from, it makes a big difference.

We're here only once, and each of us likes to do things his own way. I am not a genius who has been driven by an overriding goal. I have no goal other than to do a good job with the task at hand, whatever that may be. Every job is routine. I don't spend much time trying to decide if I like it or not; I just try to do it. I would be just as content gathering garbage, but I'd try to figure out a better way to do it.

In my case, I trace my grindstone-calloused nose to my childhood. The large ranch in Mexico provided plenty to do, and I learned young how to work hard. In Chihuahua, one of the most unpleasant jobs came during dry season, June to mid-July. During this period I and my younger brother Edward were expected to herd fifty to one hundred of the lean cattle in the alfalfa fields. Our job was to keep the cattle from eating too much in order to prevent their bloating and eventually dying. The work was not physically difficult, but it was long and tiring, and we prayed regularly for the summer rains to come to our relief.

In 1912 the Mexican revolution drove us across the border to El Paso. The five thousand or so refugees strained the town's facilities, and we spent several weeks in an unfinished house down on the riverbottom. It didn't have any windows or screening, and the mosquitoes almost carried us off. As soon as she could, mother found my younger brother and me work. I don't remember being particularly enthusiastic about this at first, but mother was a great motivator.

When father arrived, he arranged to rent a better house. Then the younger children went to school, but my brother Ed and I continued to work to help support the family. We worked at Calisher's department store as "cash boys" at $2.00 for a sixty-three-hour week. But you can't keep a good man down. By the time we left El Paso a year later, I was up to $3.50 per week. If you divide $2.00 by sixty-three hours, you get just a little over three cents per hour. Still, in 1912, in El Paso, you could buy a loaf of bread or a quart of milk for a nickel, so it helped the family quite a lot. After a short time as errand boy, I obtained work as a delivery boy at a grocery store owned by the Vinghouse family.

Each morning I would put on my roller skates, pick up my lunch pail, and head down the hill from our house to the grocery store. The interesting thing about the trip was that the sidewalk was two feet above the street, and at the bottom of the hill one had to go down steps to cross the road. However, for me it was much more of a challenge to descend the hill, then jump, going full speed, from the sidewalk into the road. In nearly every case I would fall down, losing my lunch pail in the crash. After picking up my scattered lunch, I would continue on to work. During the entire year in El Paso, I can remember only a few times that I made a successful jump, but I kept trying.

After we had lived a year in El Paso we decided that things in Mexico weren't going to settle down. Father had two wives—Romney girls—and they didn't want to go back to Mexico. Like me, he always did what his wife told him. I'm not sure just how he decided which one to obey, but he obeyed one or the other all the time.

We moved to southeastern Arizona and, after brief stays in Solomonville and Safford, Father purchased a livery stable in Thatcher. During the summer of 1914 I was given the responsibility of taking care of it. One of my duties was to rent out buggies. My best customers were the young men of Thatcher who would take a buggy to go courting their girl friends.

Sometimes your business can get you into trouble. We lived in the old academy building next to the stable. The old academy grounds had a big lot which Father, during the first week we were there, rented to a Seventh-Day Adventist preacher, to put up a tent to hold a revival meeting in this Mormon town. When I went to Sunday School, the boys said, "Ah hah! Here comes the Seventh-Day Adventist." To a Mormon boy those were fighting words. So, I asked them if they wanted to fight. They said they did. I said, "All right, it's time for Sunday School right now, but afterward let's go down by the big irrigation ditch behind the high school and we'll settle it." (Spencer W. Kimball lived right across the street from the church at that time, so I could have been in good company, but I was not making the most of my opportunities.) My Sunday School teacher was my second cousin, Lela Lee. She gave a good lesson about the apostle Paul. It wasn't really the sort of thing I needed for the business at hand, but I enjoyed it.

After Sunday School was over we went down away from the church so we wouldn't be disturbed. There were about seven boys from Thatcher, and me. It was one against seven, but it was an honorable group. They sat down on a bench—about six of them in a row. I went to Tennison Wood first and asked him if he wanted to fight. He said no. I asked about four others and they each said no, too. The last fellow, a Clarson boy, said he wanted to fight. So we fought, but I was really a little better than he was, so I put him out of business (not very seriously, but I hit him so he was pretty sure that he'd had enough). So he withdrew.

One of the boys, Barney, was sixteen years old. He decided that was not the way that sort of thing ought to end; that the local people shouldn't have their champion disposed of in that fashion; and that he'd better uphold the honor of Thatcher. I was thirteen, so he was lots bigger—big as mountains. I knew I was in trouble, but I had to fight anyway. So I rushed him as fast as I could and hit him hard with my body when he didn't expect it. This knocked him over, and I fell on top of him. That gave me a momentary advantage. But he was bigger than I was and just rolled me over so that I was under him. He pummeled my face and just made a beauty of me. My eyes were swollen practically shut and my nose was bleeding and everything. That was fine. That was the way the battle went sometimes. He had decided to teach me a lesson, which he did, although I didn't learn anything, but I should have. After he'd pounded me what he thought was enough, he let me up and I wandered on home.

When I got there, the folks were eating dinner—they hadn't waited for me. They just thought it was hilarious to see me come in with the signs of battle on me. I don't remember that much was said. I'm sure they were against a fellow fighting on the Sabbath, but I think they thought I ought to have learned something. I don't think I had, except to hit the guy harder next time. So I went back to renting buggies and reading books when I could.

One day, however, a man came in and told a lurid story about how his grandmother was dying in Pima and how he needed to go see her before she died. I let the man take a horse and saddle on the promise that he would pay me when he returned. As it turned out, he had recently gotten out of jail, and he used our horse to rob a bank in the nearby town of Wilcox. The man was caught, however, and the horse and its saddle were returned to our livery stable.

On another occasion, I had to take a man to Eden, Arizona, in a buggy, and then return to Thatcher, a distance of ten miles. On the return trip, I became lost because of my unfamiliarity with the territory. Fortunately, I ran into a young couple who had rented one of our buggies, and I followed them back to Thatcher, arriving very late that night.

In the fall of 1914 Father sold the Thatcher livery stable and bought a ninety-eight-acre farm in Pima, Arizona. This was our last move. We made the six-mile journey to Pima with all our worldly possessions and the children on a hay wagon. The adults rode in a buggy, and a cow was led behind. We made quite a procession.

The farm had only a small two-room house on it when we arrived, a bit crowded for our large family, so part of the family lived in a tent, part in the house, and the other boys and I slept in the barn. We just made our beds on the straw and corncobs in the corncrib. I remember getting up one morning and taking up my trousers to put them on and seeing a great, long centipede inside. I must say, I shook him out before I put them on.

About forty acres of the ninety-eight-acre farm were already being worked. To get the rest under cultivation, we had to clear the land of brush and mesquite. The mesquite would first have to be cut with an ax. Then we'd take a shovel and dig around the roots, and then with a pick ax chop the roots out. After we got the trees out, we'd hook a team on each end of a long, steel rail, the kind the railroad uses, and drag this rail across the land to pull out the brush, which we would burn.

Then came the plowing. The ground was baked just as hard as it could be. It was like adobe. But we had to plow it the first time before we could water it. One time, my job was to plow three acres that had never been plowed before. I had a mule and a mare hooked together on the plow, and every time the plow would bounce out of the ground, the mule and mare would start trotting, since they preferred pulling without having to pull hard. I would cry, try to slow them down so I could get the plow back in the ground, and cuss a little.

In thinking back on it later, when I'd be struggling with a particularly difficult scientific problem, I'd remember grubbing mesquite. I'd know that I could fail as a scientist and still make a living back on that farm in Arizona. There was a sense of security in that. But the memories also provided a certain incentive to succeed at my studies.

I think that those good, hard old days have helped me

with my science. I have sometimes been lazy about going to the bottom of some mathematical proposition needed in my research and have spent considerable time figuring out ways of getting along without the information. The inevitable outcome of such a course is that the particular miserable question keeps recurring until I finally dive in and clean the matter up once and for all. I then wake up surprised to discover myself on a peak with vast vistas in all directions, and I wonder why I didn't pay the honest price in the first place.

So I like to work most of the time. I don't take vacations—why should I? I give seventy-five lectures a year at many places all over the world.

To find truth, you have to try, and you have to persist in trying. Sometimes it's fun. Sometimes it's hard or boring. But it's always worth it.

# FREEDOM THROUGH OBEDIENCE

Some people stumble on the notion of obedience, but I think that obedience is the price of freedom. That may sound paradoxical—if you are tied down by rules, how can you be free? Long ago I learned how to win freedom from my regular responsibilities as a schoolteacher: by fulfilling those duties over and beyond what is required. I've taught a full course load all four quarters every year since I arrived at the University of Utah in 1946. You see, I don't even have to know the requirements because I'm already doing way more.

I learned this trick early. One day I was late for my eighth-grade class. My teacher, Miss Ledwich, said, "For being late, before you go home tonight you must recite ten verses of Gray's 'Elegy in a Country Churchyard.' I'll have you say it just when school is over." I decided that was fine; I would learn *all* of Gray's Elegy. So when we were just getting ready to go home, she said, "Henry, do you want to recite those ten verses?" I got up and recited the ten verses and then just kept going. Finally she said, "Sit down, sit down!" So, I went home with everyone else. Actually, I was just trying to indicate that I was not really rebellious—giving her full measure, and then some.

The same is true of the law of the land. If I live a higher standard than the law requires there is complete freedom from all legal strictures, and the law becomes a protecting shield against every illegal invasion of my rights by others. If I always obey the speed limits, then I don't have to own a "fuzzbuster" or keep an eye out for patrol cars. In fact, I'm glad to see them because they make me feel safer.

I don't think I ever was much impressed with the fun of being an outlaw. One incident during the same year I was in Miss Ledwich's class impressed this on me. I was a scout. I'm sure I made it all the way through Tenderfoot, and I believe I made Second Class, but I'm not quite sure. We had our regular meetings on Wednesday night. One Wednesday the scoutmaster was busy and we didn't have our scout meeting. Now, Father never thought that any of his boys should roam the streets at night, so I never did. I stayed home unless I had some specific place to go. I was allowed to go to scouting, but they didn't hold it this night.

Some of my scouting comrades wanted to climb up on Bishop Weech's movie theater. There were two buildings right together, and you could go up on one and cross over to the theater. If you lifted up some tin from the roof, you could see the movie. The theory was that Bishop Weech wouldn't care since we wouldn't have gone to the show anyway, and all we would do is just look at it, so he was just as well off as before. I knew better, but I had my image with my peers to protect.

The way they proposed getting up on the roof was to crawl up a long plank that they leaned against the twelve-foot top of the wall. It was steep. If we fell, we'd hit some very hard dirt at the bottom. I thought it was dangerous. They said, "You don't dare climb up that plank." And I didn't. I was afraid to climb it. I didn't want to see Bishop Weech's movie without paying for it. I was a physical coward, but I was even more of a moral coward. So when they dared me, I crawled up the plank on my knees, holding on for dear life.

I got up on the roof and was looking at the movie

through the hole in the roof. You could hear the tin crack for half a mile when we pulled it back. There wasn't any question about whether we advertised ourselves. We hadn't been looking at the movie for more than five minutes—there was a big moon that night; I saw that moon like I'd never seen it before—when pretty soon I saw, coming up a ladder, Brother Grover Malloy—the town marshall—and Bishop Weech. Brother Malloy came over to where we were and shone a light in our faces so he knew who we were. (He was my priesthood teacher, too.)

He arrested us and took us over to the justice of the peace, who was also my Sunday School teacher, Brother Halladay. Brother Halladay was busy right then running the dance in the pavilion, so we had to wait until quite late before we could be taken before him. It was too late to try us that night so he bound us over to appear the next day at four o'clock at his house to be tried for this wickedness of climbing up on the theater.

I went home that night a very unhappy boy. I told my father what had happened. He said, "Eyrings don't do that sort of thing. I don't know of any of our people who have had that sort of an experience before. I'm ashamed of you, but I'll help you out this time. If you ever get into this kind of a mess again, you'll have to get yourself out of it." Well, I wasn't very proud.

When the half-dozen of us got to Brother Halladay's the next day, we were ushered into his office. He had a lot of shelves just full of law books. You ought to have seen it. He'd get one law book down and look at it to find the punishment for this crime, then get another one to see what to do for that crime. Finally, after about ten or fifteen minutes just looking to see what the law was, he finally talked to us. He said, "This is a very serious matter. You're young, just boys, and I think you don't understand the gravity of this thing, but just this time we're going to let you go. If you ever do it again, you'll be in real trouble." I never felt so relieved in my life to know that I wasn't to be known as a criminal. He didn't keep any record of the trial, so we were turned free on the promise that we wouldn't ever do it again. I've steered a careful course ever since.

Natural laws require obedience, too. If you fall off your moving bicycle, the laws of gravity, momentum, and friction take their toll. Swallow poison and, unless you take the antidote, you'll suffer the consequences. The aspiring scientist must comply strictly to every detail of natural law. In no other way can he probe the mysteries of the world around him. The launching of a space probe to land on the moon or to pass by Saturn or Jupiter and photograph their surfaces and afterward relay the pictures back to earth is a triumph of painstaking and detailed obedience to natural law.

When I was about eight years old, Father bought another home in Colonia Juarez on the west side of the Piedras Verde River, right next to the Academy. One day, my friend Viv Bentley, my brother Ed, and I decided it would be interesting to hitch my little black saddle horse to our buckboard. He was a gentle horse to ride, but he hadn't been broken to pull a rig, and it scared him to death. I got into the buckboard after I'd harnessed him and put him inside, and he took off like he'd been shot from a gun. I could keep him slowed down at first, so that we got out through the gate all right onto the main road, but then he started running. He was so scared I couldn't hold him. I hadn't gone very far when he went across a ditch. That threw me out of the seat against the end-gate in front of me, and, trying to catch myself, I lost the reins. So then he was just running free down the street as fast as he could go. As we went across the high school grounds my Uncle Thomas, mother's brother, says he yelled, "Jump! Jump!" But I didn't hear him. I was just watching the horse. I couldn't have jumped anyway. I was just trying to hang on. I didn't know how it was going to end, but I knew that hitting the ground at that speed would not be much fun.

A man by the name of Earl Header had his horse right there on the grounds where he and some friends were playing baseball. He got onto his horse and came riding after me. The horse had been running away for about four city blocks, about half a mile, and he turned a corner and went up a street, then turned another corner in about two blocks, then turned another corner and headed off for the fields. I was beginning to wonder where I would spend the night, if he went all the way to the ranch. I didn't have to worry, because Earl came riding up on his horse (he was an excellent horseman), reached over and got the reins, wrapped them around his saddlehorn, and slowed his own horse down, and that stopped my horse.

When we got back, the men decided they'd teach the horse not to run away, so they put a man in the buggy, let the horse start a little bit, and then pulled back on him and even threw him down. I told them not to do that. I liked that horse, and had no ill will against him. I had the feeling that he was just scared, and I thought he did just what he ought to under the circumstances. I was the one who didn't obey the rules of handling horses, and he was getting punished.

I thought no more about deserving punishment until in the morning, in devotional at school, when Aunt Ann, one of my mother's sisters who was the principal of the school, got up right after the opening song and prayer and, in a trembling voice, spoke of seeing her sweet little nephew—she hadn't realized until then how much she loved him—almost killed. It was awful. The embarrassment of that moment was punishment enough.

The summer after my junior year in mining engineering at the University of Arizona, I got work at the Inspiration Copper Company in Miami, Arizona. I found out that Newton was dead wrong. He said that apples fall on your head, but it turned out to be rocks. And that impressed me. Once I was working as a timberman, and a large rock fell on my left foot. My boot filled partially with blood, and I was on the disabled list for a time. During another shift I worked, three men were killed in three separate accidents. I was just smart enough to realize that that wasn't particularly the way I wanted to die, so I changed professions. Even though, as a mining engineer, I wouldn't have had to go down into the mines myself, I didn't want to send anyone else down there, either. I obeyed my own "natural law": If it scares you, don't do it.

In the spiritual realm, the attainment of any blessing is predicated upon obedience to the laws that govern that blessing. (See D&C 130:20–21.) The Prophet Joseph Smith was surpassed by some in secular learning, but he was unsurpassed by anyone in his humble willingness to learn. He was genuinely teachable and was always willing to yield obedience to the promptings of the Spirit. Obedience to gospel principles can make man master of himself, and thus of his own destiny. There is no greater freedom than this.

Obedience to the laws of health, including the Word of Wisdom, frees man from the restrictions that come from bodily ills. Tobacco is filthy. If I had to smoke to be a member of the Church, I suppose I'd make the sacrifice, but I'd surely feel imposed upon. Alcohol is much the same thing. A lot of people are so bright that they have to dull their senses with alcohol in order to be on a par with the rest of us. Well, I start at a low enough level that I don't have that problem. I'm dumb enough and make mistakes on my own.

Once I was in an informal discussion of longevity with some medical school faculty members. One of the doctors mentioned statistics that indicated that moderate drinkers live longer than teetotalers and remarked, "So you see, Henry, we are going to live longer than you." I replied, "But I am going to a better place."

Being a member of the Church is no sacrifice. People come up to me and say, "You're a scientist; isn't it wonderful that you're a member of the Church." I say, "I'm just trying to look after my own hide." I don't have to be noble. I'm just smart enough to try to take care of my own interests. There isn't a thing I'm expected to do in the Church that isn't the best thing for me.

I can understand that some people might want to see football on Sunday. In gladiatorial combat they were even crueler; they killed each other. In football all they do is cripple each other so that they can't pray. They wreck their knees so that at best they have to pray standing up. I want to be able to kneel down to pray. I don't have to make any sacrifice to be a member of the Church.

When I obey good rules and wise laws, even a little better than I'm required to do, other people leave me alone, and I'm free to do those good and right things that the best part of me wants to do anyway.

# SCIENCE ENHANCES RELIGION

In the autumn of 1957, in Houston, Texas, the Welch Foundation invited the top nuclear physicists and chemists from all over the world to a symposium. At a dinner, twelve of the most distinguished were seated at a table. As one of the scientific advisors to the Welch Foundation, I was privileged to attend. Mr. Malone, as trustee of the foundation, said, "Dr. Eyring, how many of these gentlemen believe in a Supreme Being?" I answered, "I don't know, but I'll ask."

I asked if all were willing to answer the question. All agreed. The question was then formulated precisely: "Which best expresses your point of view: that there is a Supreme Being or that there is not a Supreme Being?"

So I asked these twelve scientists, and every one said, "I believe." All of these students of the exact sciences saw in the universal order about them evidence for a Supreme Being. Two of the twelve had the Nobel Prize, and the other ten felt they should have the Nobel Prize too, so it was a very distinguished group.

The result was interesting to me. To explain this unanimity, the following seems important. Exact scientists are deeply impressed by the precision with which natural laws apply. Any explanation that ignores a Planner leaves this precision unexplained and is therefore unacceptable. I think scientists from other disciplines further removed from the exact sciences might not have voted with such unanimity.

Now, of course, the scientist is not usually a specialist in questions of religion. But that need not mean that he is not a believer in the great principles of Christianity. Many of the noted pioneers in the scientific world were men of faith whose learning in their chosen fields seemed only to strengthen their sense of a great spiritual realm beyond their ken.

For example, Archimedes, Newton, and Gauss are usually ranked first among the great mathematicians.

About Archimedes' religious ideas very little is known, but the other two have revealed their attitudes. Touching on Newton's position, the mathematician E. T. Bell, in his book *Men of Mathematics*, says, "Newton was an unquestioning believer in an all-wise Creator of the universe."

The great mathematician Gauss indicated his view when he said, "There are problems to whose solution I would attach infinitely greater importance than to those of mathematics; for example, touching ethics, or our relation to God, or concerning our destiny and our future."

It would be folly, of course, to maintain that all men who have achieved eminence in the scientific world have been religious men. La Place, one of the very great physicists, when asked by Napoleon why his great book on the origin of the universe failed to mention Deity, said, "Sire, I have no need for that hypothesis." That is another point of view. But I think that most scientists have had the humility and the frankness to acknowledge that there are religious forces in the lives of men that are both real and potent, although they, the scientists, may have had no personal acquaintance with the forces within their own experiences.

Most scientists, I believe, would not presume to say that a thing may not be because they do not understand it, nor would they deny the validity of the spiritual experiences of others because they have been without such experiences themselves.

I am now going to venture to say that science has rendered a service to religion. The scientific spirit is a spirit of inquiry, a spirit of reaching out for truth. In the final analysis, this spirit is the essence of religion. The Savior said, "Ask, and it shall be given you; seek, and ye shall find; knock, and it shall be opened unto you." (Matthew 7:7.) The scientist has, in effect, reaffirmed this great fundamental laid down by the Master, and in doing so has given a new impetus to religion.

Science has also strengthened religion by helping to sift the grain of truth from the chaff of fable. The philosopher William James is reported to have told a story about a woman who came to one of his lectures and explained to him that the earth is flat and rests on the back of a giant turtle. He asked, "What is the turtle standing on?" "On the back of a still bigger turtle," came the reply. He started to ask the obvious question when the woman held up her hand and said, "Never mind, it's turtles, all the way down."

That would have occurred around the turn of the century, and you might think that such ideas have changed, particularly in our age of satellites and space travel, with pictures of a round earth taken from space. But every year or so the newspapers remind us of the continued existence of the Flat Earth Society. Its president was recently reported to have described a flight of the Columbia space shuttle as a "continuing giant ripoff of the taxpayers of America." According to him, the Columbia couldn't have orbited the earth, since the earth is flat. It landed at sea a few minutes after it took off, being kept afloat by "those big tanks." The films purportedly taken from space were done in a studio, and the spectacular landing was accomplished by hauling the shuttle aloft and dropping it over the desert air base.

There was a time when many people thought that the pure understanding of the scriptures required the acceptance of a flat earth. The Bible speaks of the four corners of the earth and of the stars in the firmament, conjuring up the image of lights on the inside of a giant dome covering the earth. In the time of Columbus, many people thought a flat earth was a religious necessity. When it turned out to be round, Christ's teachings were found to be just as consistent with the new view as with the old. In fact, the great underlying principles of faith were brought into bolder relief when the clutter of false notions was removed from around them.

Sometimes science has at first appeared to be at odds with religion, but then new discoveries have come to provide supporting insight. For example, during my lifetime we have been obliged to give up the old determinism of classical mechanics as well as the idea of the indestructibility of matter. Mechanical determinism meant that if a sufficiently expert mathematician were given the state of the universe at any instant of time, he could calculate the state of things at all times to come. This left no place for the great religious principle of free will. Then quantum mechanics brought with it the uncertainty principle. This principle eliminates the possibility of predicting the future exactly, and tends to confirm the fundamental Christian tenet that man enjoys agency as a divine gift.

The atomic bomb dramatically emphasized a fact discovered earlier in relativity theory and in laboratory experiments—matter can disappear only to reappear again as energy. This liberalization in our conceptions regarding matter gives added significance to the doctrine that the spirit is composed of a refined kind of matter.

And so, if you are a man or woman of religion, look to the sciences for insights and methods for uncovering still more truths, realizing that ultimately all truths are in harmony. If you are a young person who may feel inclined to disparage religion as you pursue other studies, you will bring enrichment to your life by cultivating faith and an interest in things of the spirit as you follow your other pursuits. Such faith will never detract from your abilities in other fields, but it will broaden your thinking and give added depth to your character.

It is important that all men of good will use their energies, their talents, and their learning in their chosen fields to help build a better world.

# WARTS AND SKELETONS

The Church was planning the new Church magazines, which would begin to appear in 1971. As a member of the Sunday School General Board I got a letter from Richard L. Evans, a member of the Quorum of the Twelve, to come to a meeting about the new magazines along with a great many other people. The night before the meeting, I was visiting my sister Camilla and her husband, Spencer W. Kimball, and I said, "I am going to a meeting for the magazines." Spencer said, "I am going, too, at nine o'clock." In the morning, my secretary was gone, and I was a little bit late, so I hurried down to the Church Office Building. I went in and said to the receptionist that I was supposed to go to a meeting. He said, "Well, isn't it this afternoon?" I said, "No, it's this morning." And so he took me in and there were four apostles—Spencer W. Kimball, Marion G. Romney, Brother Evans, and Howard W. Hunter—and the magazine editors. I was quite surprised that no one else was there from the Sunday School, but I thought, "Well, they must regard me very highly," and so I just sat down. The discussion went around, and I was willing to offer my view quite freely. However, Brother Evans said, "Your turn will come in a few minutes."

When they got around to me, I told them that the Church magazines never would amount to a darn if they did not get some people with independence in there who had real ideas and would come out and express themselves. If they were going to rehash old stuff, they would not hold the young people. I gave them quite a bit of very fine advice and I cussed a little when I wanted to, and when I got through, Brother Evans said, "I do not know anyone who characterizes the idea of independence any more than you do. Are you applying for the job?" I said, "No, I am not applying for the job, but I think I have given good advice."

I did not have any feeling, even after I had been there, that anything was wrong, and thought that they must have a high opinion of my wisdom. When I got back to my office, my secretary asked, "Where have you been?" I said I had been down to the Church magazine meeting. She said, "That is this afternoon at two o'clock."

What is so funny is not that I made a mistake, but that I was so insensitive as to not realize it. I didn't go to the two o'clock meeting. I felt I had done my work. Brother Evans got up in that meeting and, I am told, said that they had had a meeting in the morning and that very useful advice had been supplied by Brother Eyring. He did not say I had not been invited.

I was amazed at the graciousness of the Brethren in making me feel I belonged, when any one of them might well have been annoyed. They are a most urbane group. On my part, there was no holding back; I just tried to help them all I could.

However, the point I was making at that meeting still interests me. We should be willing to enjoy a full picture of our heroes, leaders, and history. I believe that when we ignore the "darker side" we leave ourselves unprepared for the revelation of some unhappy deed or event of past or present. We might be better off if we leave the warts on and let a few of the skeletons out of the closets ourselves for open examination. On the other hand, there are dangers in debunking everyone and everything that is a little above the ordinary. We ought to seek a happy balance of letting the truth flow forth without either hiding or digging for problems.

For example, I believe the biography of my brother-in-law, President Spencer W. Kimball, is excellent. It portrays a mortal, such as I am, struggling to do the best he can. I know him well, and everything I know about him is good. I admire him a great deal, and his biography helped me appreciate him even more. It showed that even while he was doing more than almost anyone else has ever done, he still worried about whether it was enough. He may have even done a "human" thing or two. How wonderful! That helps me admire even more the magnificent leader he is.

I've often said that I would be delighted to have someone point out some flaw in the Book of Mormon that proved that Joseph Smith made an error in translating or inserted some idea of his own that wasn't on the plates. Of course, he might have been inspired to deviate. But even if I thought otherwise, that would merely prove that he was human, a fact about which I was already quite sure. It would also show that the Creator is tolerant of a mistake now and then. These seem quite hopeful ideas to me, since I am clearly human and have made at least my full share of mistakes.

An example of what I am talking about is the recent discovery of the papyrus scrolls from which Joseph Smith was presumed to have translated the book of Abraham in the Pearl of Great Price. Modern scholars, looking at the scrolls, found nothing they considered to be similar to that book. I remarked at the time that such a finding didn't bother me in the least. God doesn't need a crib sheet in the form of a papyrus scroll to reveal Abraham's thoughts and words to Joseph Smith, with any degree of precision He considers necessary for His purposes. If the only function of the scrolls was to awaken the Prophet to the idea of receiving such inspiration, they would have fulfilled their purpose.

Scientists don't know everything about every topic either. I suspect that if I asked you to name a scientist, you would first think of Albert Einstein. Certainly he was an extraordinarily able man, but he didn't know everything.

I went to Princeton in '31. Einstein came in '33. I left in '46, so we overlapped thirteen years. In all that time I think I talked with him about ten hours. Obviously, he had other things to do than chat with me. You would have thought that with the charm I have that he would have wanted to talk to me all the time, but it didn't work out that way.

On one such occasion a man from the Navy and I spent the morning with Einstein at his home talking about high explosives. I think he was more interested in relativity than high explosives, but he was not a bad chemist. He didn't talk sense all the time because he had been studying astronomy and physics and such things. At noon we walked out into what had been a rose garden, but in wartime had been replanted as a victory garden. Now, I'm a farmer from Pima, so I guessed what the crop was, but I didn't know whether Einstein knew or not. So I picked up a plant and asked him what it was. He didn't know. We walked about a hundred yards to where the gardener was sitting on his wheelbarrow. As I walked by, I asked him what it was. He said, "They're soybeans." Well, I thought what you would have thought: "Einstein doesn't know beans." More than that, he had walked past that crop four times a day since it had been planted, and it was now ready to harvest. So there wasn't much hope that he would ever know, which is kind of a pitiful thing. But he knew everything else. He was just weak on beans.

Albert Einstein and I, along with everyone else, may have some foibles and weaknesses. These should be happily admitted, while at the same time giving due credit and appreciation for what valuable contributions are made. Let's tell it like it is, with adequate positive emphasis. Let's leave the warts and examine the skeletons.

Now, I'm not sure I was right about what should be done with the Church magazines. Perhaps the more inquisitive and sometimes not quite comfortable side of truth shouldn't be explored in official Church publications by Church employees or leaders. But I think there is a place for such inquiry when conducted as responsible scholarship.

I have one caution about scholarship as it relates to the Church, its history, leaders, and doctrines. We need to be continually reminded that however interesting some such topic might be, it has no relevance to religious faith, one way or the other. You can't intellectualize your way to a testimony. There will always be another question beyond the one you have just answered. Incidentally, the same is true of science. None of its findings are final. Still, some people seem to stumble when they run into a contradiction.

I have trouble understanding why people drift away from the Church. I'm sure the reasons are different and varied. I can understand if a person wants to misbehave and has to rationalize to himself. He has to think he's all right. But I also understand that people who think they have to be as smart as the Lord, understand everything, and have no contradictions in their minds may have trouble. There are all kinds of contradictions that I don't understand, but I find the same kinds of contradictions in science, and I haven't decided to apostatize from science.

In the long run, the truth is its own most powerful advocate. The Lord uses imperfect people. He often allows their errors to stand uncorrected. He may have a purpose in doing so, such as to teach us that religious truth comes forth "line upon line, precept upon precept" in a process of sifting and winnowing similar to the one I know so well in science.

# THE SCRIPTURES

The scriptures record God's dealing with his prophets, and they are as accurate as God, in his wisdom, requires. They are particularly important in showing us how to live and treat one another. Such injunctions for living as "Love thy neighbor as thyself" are powerful tools in the hands of believers for shaping a better world. We can study the scriptures long and hard every day and still be struggling with the practical application of these great principles in our lives.

My family and I were having dinner one night with Spencer and Camilla. The doorbell interrupted us at one point, and Spencer went to give some time (and apparently substance as well) to a caller.

This prompted me, upon his return, to relate an experience with a visitor in my home of a few nights earlier. This fellow was an apparently destitute member of a minority group who had come to see me about once a year for the previous two or three years. He always had a wonderfully sorry story to tell and would introduce me to his wife or other companions and ask if I could help him out. One year I gave him my sweater and some money, and other years just money.

On this most recent occasion, however, alcohol had rendered him decidedly strong of breath and wobbly of gait, and his "wife" was not the same one as in the previous year. I gave him twenty dollars and sent him on his way with the stern admonition that he shouldn't come back again. (Indeed, I've not seen him since, and this was twenty years ago.)

The conversation turned to the particularly troublesome scripture in this regard in Mosiah: "And ye will not suffer that the beggar putteth up his petition to you in vain, and turn him out to perish. Perhaps thou shalt say: The man has brought upon himself his misery; therefore I will stay my hand, and will not give unto him of my food, nor impart unto him of my substance that he may not suffer, for his punishments are just—But I say unto you, O man, whosoever doeth this the same hath great cause to repent; and except he repenteth of that which he hath done he perisheth forever, and hath no interest in the kingdom of God." (Mosiah 4:16–18.)

I asked Spencer what he thought of my chances and how he dealt with that particular scripture, since he must have a never-ending stream of such visitors. His eyes twinkled, and he smiled slightly as he said, "I always read fast when I get to those verses." He didn't mean it, of course. I don't know anyone who comes closer to meeting the high standard of that scripture than Spencer, but it's nice to know that he understands the rest of us.

The scriptures set a high standard for the ways we should treat each other. In addition to teaching us how to live and relate to one another, the scriptures give us insight into the system of rules and laws within which God works and relates to us: "Strait is the gate, and narrow is the way, which leadeth unto life, and few there be that find it." (Matthew 7:14.) "Except a man be born of water and of the Spirit, he cannot enter into the kingdom of God." (John 3:5.) Apparently, even God is subject to the laws of justice and mercy: "What, do ye suppose that mercy can rob justice? I say unto you, Nay; not one whit. If so, God would cease to be God." (Alma 42:25.) The scriptures teach us, therefore, that it isn't enough to be good neighbors and honest with our fellowmen and do all other good and kind things. We must also be obedient and conform to the prescribed ordinances of the gospel, such as baptism and the temple ceremonies.

I was baptized a member of the Church by John C. Harper, a veteran of the Civil War, in the Piedras Verde River, which flowed through Colonia Juarez, where I lived. Brother Harper was a fine old gentleman whom we all admired and who performed most of the baptisms there. Father confirmed me a member of the Church the following Sunday.

Christ himself was baptized "to fulfill all righteousness." (Matthew 3:15.)

God has told us that the scriptures are incomplete. We are promised that we will receive more when we have mastered the lessons of what we have. Hence, teaching us how to live and treat others and how to obey the rules and laws of the gospel is the primary purpose of the scriptures; they are spiritual guides to religious questions. Of course, the scriptures do treat incidentally scientific, historical, and other nonreligious questions. In these areas, they should be supplemented by all relevant information. Viewed in this light, most problems disappear. I am obliged, as a Latter-day Saint, to believe whatever is true, regardless of the source. Questions involving the age of the earth, pre-Adamic man, or organic evolution may seem to us to be interesting and important. However, I doubt that God thinks they matter enough to have provided definitive explanations in our current scriptures. They will all receive adequate answers in due course. Whatever the ultimate answers are, the gospel will remain, and new questions will take the place of those we solve. For me, the truth of the gospel does not hinge on such questions, interesting as they are.

# THE AGE OF THE EARTH

When President Joseph Fielding Smith's book *Man, His Origin and Destiny* was published, someone urged it as an institute course. One of the institute teachers came to me and said, "If we have to follow it exactly, we will lose some of the young people." I said, "I don't think you need to worry." I thought it was a good idea to get this problem out in public, so the next time I went to Sunday School General Board meeting, I got up and bore my testimony that the evidence was strongly in the direction that the world was four or five billion years old. That week, President Smith called and asked me to come see him. We talked for about an hour, and he explained his views to me. I said, "Brother Smith, I have read your books and know your point of view, and I understand that is how it looks to you. It just looks a little different to me." He said as we ended, "Well, Brother Eyring, I would like to have you come in and let me talk with you sometime when you are not quite so excited." As far as I could see, we parted on the best of terms.

I would say that I sustained President Smith as my Church leader one hundred percent. I think he was a great man. He had a different background and training on this issue. Maybe he was right. I think he was right on most things, and if you followed him, he would get you into the celestial kingdom.

The scriptures record God's dealing with his children

back to a "beginning" some six thousand years ago, but dismiss the long prologue in a few short paragraphs. The scriptures tell us of six creative periods followed by a period of rest. During these periods the earth was organized and took essentially its present form. In the King James Version of the Bible, the phrase *creative periods* is rendered as "days." The use of this term has led to at least three interpretations. In the first, the "days" are construed to mean the usual day of twenty-four hours. In the second, the days of creation are interpreted as thousand-year periods following such statements as occur in 2 Peter 3:8: "One day is with the Lord as a thousand years, and a thousand years as one day." The third interpretation accepts "creative periods" as times of unspecified length and looks to a study of the earth itself to give added meaning to the exceedingly brief scriptural accounts.

In earlier times some variation of the first two interpretations was all but universally held by the Christian world. This is no longer true. In school and in secular publications, the third interpretation is the generally accepted one. Accordingly, whatever our own point of view may be, we need to know the viewpoint presented to our children if we are to be effective counselors to them.

The cumulative thickness of rocks laid down as sediment is about four hundred fifty thousand feet, or eighty miles. The rate of deposition varies enormously with the time and the place, but a not unreasonable average rate is one foot every 250 years. This leads to a very rough estimate of 112 million years for the time required to deposit all the known sediments.

Also, in my opinion, the orderly structure of these horizontally lying layers, with their fossils, argues strongly against the notion that the earth has been assembled, relatively recently, from the wreckage of earlier worlds.

A quantitative way of getting at the age of strata and other earth structures is by use of the radioactive decay of various elements. An analogy of how radioactive decay works may be helpful. If one should look at a fire and note that half the wood is burned the first hour and that an hour after that, half of what was left had burned, he could say the fire obeys the radioactive decay law. This law states that in a given length of time the same fraction of the fuel is burned, independent of the circumstances. Conversely, by measuring the fuel remaining at a fire and the amount of ashes already produced, one can deduce the fraction of the fuel consumed and so estimate how long the fire has been burning.

All the radioactive elements behave like our hypothetical fire in that, independent of the existing conditions, the same fraction of the radioactive elements is always transformed to another element in a given interval of time. The new element is the ashes of the radioactive fire; for example, half of the potassium (atomic weight forty) present to begin with changes into argon forty in a period of 1,300 million years, and half of what remains is changed in the next 1,300 million years, and so on. This period of 1,300 million years is called the half-life of potassium forty.

When a potassium-containing mineral crystallizes, it is ordinarily free of all gaseous argon. As time goes on, the potassium forty changes to argon forty at a rate determined by its half-life. If the crystal doesn't leak so that the liberated argon is retained inside the crystal, one can melt the crystal, measure the amount of potassium and the amount of argon, and so determine the age of the crystal.

If equal amounts of argon forty and potassium forty are found, the crystallization occurred 1,300 million years ago. If there is only one part potassium to three parts argon, 2,600 million years have elapsed since crystallization of the mineral occurred, and so on. Clearly, any potassium-containing mineral constitutes a built-in clock that we can use to read the time of the formation of the crystalline mineral.

Many complications may arise to make the clock give incorrect time. If some argon was entrapped in the crystal as it formed, the clock will read too long a time. If some of the argon has escaped since crystallization occurred, the indicated time will be too short. Nonetheless, by being careful to choose elements with appropriate half-lives and by careful selection of the crystal used and by using more than one kind of a "clock," a reasonably consistent time scale for the formation of the various strata in the world has been achieved.

The radioactive clocks, together with the orderly way many sediments containing fossils are laid down, result in agreement by most scientists on an age for the earth of about four-and-one-half billion years. On the other hand, the exact age of the earth is apparently of so little import religiously that the scriptures sketch earth history in only the briefest terms. The present heated religious controversies on the subject will undoubtedly be resolved in time and will then appear as quaint as the medieval arguments on the shape of the earth seem to us now.

In my judgment, anyone who denies the orderly deposition of sediments with their built-in radioactive clocks places himself in a scientifically untenable position. Actually, the antiquity of the earth was no problem for two of our greatest Latter-day Saint leaders and scientists, John A. Widtsoe and James E. Talmage. However, there are vast differences in the training and background of members of the Church. Therefore, I am completely content that there is room in the Church for people who think that the periods of creation were twenty-four hours, one thousand years, or millions of years. I think it is fine to discuss these questions and for each individual to try to convert others to what he thinks is right. It is only fair to warn parents and teachers that a young person is going to face a very substantial body of scientific evidence supporting the earth's age as millions of years, and that a young person might "throw the baby out with the bath" unless allowed to seek the truth, from whatever source, without prejudice.

The Lord made the world in some wonderful way that I can at best only dimly comprehend. It seems to me sacrilegious to presume that I can really understand him and know just how he did it. He can only tell me in figurative speech that I dimly understand, but that I expect to more completely comprehend in the eternities to come. He created the world, and my faith does not hinge on the detailed procedures he used.

# ORGANIC EVOLUTION

When one of my grandsons was a small boy, just starting Primary, someone remarked to him, "So, now you are a Sunbeam." His face clouded, and he answered, "I am not a 'unbeam, I'm Henry Johnson Eyring!" I can understand how we sometimes object to being labeled. Some labels we accept. For instance, I'm content with "Mormon," "devout," "Christian," "chemist," "husband," "father," and so forth. Sometimes, however, a label is loaded with emotional baggage far beyond its usefulness or importance. For example, "organic evolutionist" or "creationist" are labels, either one of which I would reject, for myself, at least. They simply carry too much baggage and confusion for my taste.

Considering the difference in training of the members of the Church, I never cease to marvel at the degree of agreement found among believing Latter-day Saints. However, organic evolution is one topic upon which there is apt to be wide disagreement.

Such a topic becomes controversial partly because it is interesting to us, but it seems to be sufficiently nonessential to our salvation that the Creator has only briefly treated it in the scriptures. If you think about it, it makes almost no difference at all to the way we should live our lives and treat one another. Still, there are those who line up on both sides as if everything depended on the outcome of this year's "monkey trial."

Some people object to the slightest hint of being related to the rest of the animal kingdom, particularly the hairy apes. The idea is right next to the three "s's"—spiders, snakes, and sharks—on their list of things beyond the pale. I've never had that particular aversion. In fact, I've kind of enjoyed what little I've seen of them.

One time I was stuck most of a day in London and couldn't face the thought of sightseeing, so I went to the London Zoo. I was attracted by a crowd watching the great apes. One fellow in particular was getting a lot of attention as he sat close to the front of the cage on a tree platform. As the zoo visitors moved closer, he suddenly spewed them with water he had in his mouth. Now, that was interesting! I found a bench across the path—out of range—and watched. The ape got down and went over to his water trough to reload. He then went about the cage awhile and finally repositioned himself on the platform. He waited—patiently. Finally a new group of humanoids, not aware of the danger, moved into range. Spray! Splat! Bullseye! The fellow practically chortled out loud as he made his trip to the trough. I spent the entire afternoon enjoying his enjoyment. Theoretically, he was there for our amusement, but quite clearly, he didn't understand that. He thought we were there for his. I have to admit I kind of admired the fellow. Animals seem pretty wonderful to me. I'd be content to discover that I share a common heritage with them, so long as God is at the controls.

I have always felt comfortable with the views of our trained scientists among the General Authorities. For example, James E. Talmage delivered a sermon entitled "The Earth and Man" from the Salt Lake Tabernacle on August 9, 1931, and John A. Widtsoe published "Science and the Gospel" in the Young Men's Mutual Improvement Association manual of 1908–9. Each of these brethren regarded the earth as having a very great age and were open to the testimony of science to uncover the truth on those questions.

What, then, is to prevent us from seeking to understand God's methods of creation by any and all means available to us? Many avoid seeking understanding from science because they believe that any theory in conflict with the Lord's revelations will finally be proven false. Of course, given those assumptions, the position is clearly correct, since I don't believe that God intentionally misleads his children.

We have a dilemma, however, because God has left messages all over in the physical world that scientists have learned to read. These messages are quite clear, well-understood, and accepted in science. That is, the theories that the earth is about four-and-one-half billion years old and that life evolved over the last billion years or so are as well established scientifically as many theories ever are. So, if the word of God found in the scriptures and the word of God found in the rocks are contradictory, must we choose between them, or is there some way they can be reconciled?

The scriptures state that Adam was the first man on the earth and that he was also the first flesh. Other scriptures teach that Adam was not subject to mortal and spiritual death before the fall, and that the fall brought these deaths into the world. Also, the scriptures say the earth is passing through seven periods ("days") of temporal existence, and that it was not temporal before the fall. Each of these ideas seems to be in conflict with the scientific views of organic evolution, but are they?

The fundamental principle that has guided my religious life is that I need believe only what is true. The gospel is the truth as learned or discovered by whatever means and tools I can lay my hand or mind on. I appreciate the scriptures for their insights into how to love God and my neighbor and how to learn obedience to the laws and ordinances of the gospel. These teachings are precious to all devoted Latter-day Saints. However, the brevity of the scriptures about

God's methods of creation indicates that this may be a subject we will understand sometime but do not need to worry about for the time being: "Yea, verily I say unto you, in that day when the Lord shall come, he shall reveal all things—things which have passed, and hidden things which no man knew, things of the earth, by which it was made, and the purpose and the end thereof—things most precious, things that are above, and things that are beneath, things that are in the earth, and upon the earth, and in heaven." (D&C 101:32–34.)

In the meantime, I think it is perfectly appropriate for us to study and learn as much as we can about this wonderful place God has prepared for us.

We should keep in mind that scientists are as diligent and truthful as anyone else. Organic evolution is the honest result of capable people trying to explain the evidence to the best of their ability. From my limited study of the subject I would say that the physical evidence supporting the theory is considerable from a scientific viewpoint.

In my opinion it would be a very sad mistake if a parent or teacher were to belittle scientists as being wicked charlatans or else fools having been duped by half-baked ideas that gloss over inconsistencies. That isn't an accurate assessment of the situation, and our children or students will be able to see that when they begin their scientific studies.

"Now wait a minute," you say. "I thought you weren't an 'evolutionist'!" I'm not. I'd be just as content to find out that God stirred up some dirt and water and out stepped Adam, ready to occupy the Garden of Eden. The only important thing is that God did it. I might say in that regard that in my mind the theory of evolution has to include a notion that the dice have been loaded from the beginning in favor of more complex life forms. That is, without intelligent design of the natural laws in such a way as to favor evolution from lower forms to higher forms of life, I don't think the theory holds water. I can't see randomly generated natural laws producing these remarkable results. So, in my mind, God is behind it all whether we evolved or not.

Probably one of the most difficult problems in reading the scriptures is to decide what is to be taken literally and what is figurative. In this connection, it seems to me that the Creator must operate with facts and with an understanding that goes entirely outside our understanding and our experience. Because of this, when someone builds up a system of logic, however careful and painstaking, that gives a positive answer to this difficult question, I can't help but wonder about it, particularly if it seems to run counter to the Creator's revelations written in the physical world. At least I would like to move slowly in such matters.

The really awful thing about me is that I really don't care one way or the other. Sometime, a billion years from now, it may come up in some heavenly science class and I'll be glad to know, but until then I'll be content.

# THE PHYSICAL WORLDS

My wife and I have a lot that is sixty feet across the front, one hundred feet deep, and extends straight up to the limits of space, so far as I know. Clearly, this qualifies me to speak on the broader aspects of the universe.

We live in a series of six worlds, from the infinitesimally small to the infinitely big. They can be represented by a point surrounded by five circles. This chapter deals with the five physical worlds of the nucleus, atom, living cell, everyday experience, and stars. The next chapter explores the sixth, the spiritual world.

The first, or central, world is the world of the atomic nucleus. The nucleus is where most of the weight of the atom is situated. One hundred thousand atomic nuclei touching each other in a line extend only across one atom, and it takes 100 million atoms to make one inch! Vibrations inside the nuclei of atoms are about a million times more frequent than the vibrations between atoms.

It is natural to wonder how anything as small as the nucleus can have structure, and even if it does, how we can find out about it. The procedure for finding out is to shoot electrically charged atoms or electrons at nuclei and see how they bounce. This tells us a great deal about the kinds of forces that are acting between the colliding particles.

When a particularly violent collision results in penetration into the nucleus and causes it to fragment, we can watch the tracks left by the fragments in a cloud chamber. In this way we find out that the nucleus is made up of positively charged protons and uncharged neutrons of virtually the same weight.

For twenty-five years scientists accepted *parity,* the principle that an atom does not know which end is up and has the same properties in all directions. However, an experiment suggested by Yang and Lee, for which they were given the Nobel Prize, showed otherwise. If we put radioactive cobalt sixty in a magnetic field, its nuclei line up with their south poles pointing toward the north pole of the earth. Every once in a while, one of the cobalt nuclei shoots out an electron. If the nuclei were indeed symmetrical, they would be equally likely to eject the electron through the north pole as through the south pole. However, a Geiger counter, similar to those used to prospect for uranium, reveals that the electrons are shot out preferentially through the nuclear south pole. Thus, the principle of parity must be given up.

Now the scientists have introduced *quarks*, fractional particles having a charge of one-third. When quarks were proposed in the early 1970s, they were conceived of as being undivided particles, although their charge was fractional. More recently observations have indicated the existence of one-dimensional conductors called *solitons*, which have fractional charge and fractional electron number.

By such experiments we come to understand something of the complexity and intricacy of this almost unimaginably tiny world of the nucleus. One hesitates to speculate whether we have even yet found the indivisible building blocks of the physical world.

The second world is the world of chemistry, made up of atoms and molecules. This, too, is a tiny world. It would take 100 million atoms placed side by side to make an inch. A molecule finishes one of its vibrations in about a ten million millionth of a second. We call this length of time a *jiffy* for lack of a better name. The quartz-crystal watch you wear on your wrist derives its great accuracy from such rapid vibrations.

An example of the exactness with which the universe works is found in the ammonia molecule. Ammonia consists of a nitrogen atom sitting on three hydrogen atoms. The startling fact is that this umbrella-like molecule turns wrong-side out almost twenty-four thousand million times a second. If you beam radar through a tube containing ammonia, the signal fades just when the radar frequency equals the inversion frequency of the molecules. In this way the ammonia molecules can be used as a clock to break time up into twenty-four thousand millionths of a second with unprecedented accuracy. It is interesting that this ammonia molecule turns wrong-side out just as often whether it is at room temperature or at the lowest temperature obtainable in the laboratory; whether in Soviet Russia or the United States; and whether this country is Democratic or Republican. Many things we think are important don't seem to affect the ammonia molecule much. The accuracy and order of the universe continue without regard to fashions in hairstyles, clothes, politics, science, or religion. What's true is true. What works, works.

When I went to Berkeley in 1925 to take my Ph.D., no one could explain more than a tenth of the attraction of two hydrogen atoms for each other. We knew that each hydrogen atom was uncharged, being made up of a positive nucleus whose charge was just neutralized by the charge on a negative electron. True, the atoms could distort each other and give about one-tenth of the observed binding energy, but the remaining part of the bond was a mystery.

The complete answer supplied by quantum mechanics was that the electron pair, by keeping out of the way of each other as they circulated around the two nuclei, could spend enough time between the two positive nuclei to glue them together to just the observed amount.

In order for the pair of bonded atoms to exchange partners with a similar pair, thus making a new compound, the pairs must approach each other closely. Accordingly, as two pairs of bonded atoms bump into each other, they can only approach and change partners if one or the other pair of electrons are pushed out of the way into an upper state. This collisional work that has to be done so a chemical reaction can take place is called the *energy of activation*.

Using this picture of the energy of activation accompanying a chemical reaction and building on the labors of my many able predecessors, it was possible for me, in 1935, to write down the general equation for the rate of all chemical reactions. This equation has become an integral part of chemistry, used universally.

The excitement of standing, in imagination, at a pass between two energy valleys representing the initial and final states in a chemical reaction and counting the activated complexes as they make their way over the pass in shattering collisions in which atoms are exchanged between the two colliding molecules is the thrill of a lifetime.

Further, to find that wave mechanics and thermodynamics, which have had so many other triumphs, are the same tools that enable us to quantitatively explain this all-pervading aspect of the material world in which we live brings a feeling of awe at the order and exactness of the universe that is never forgotten.

The third world in which we live is the world of the living cell, the world of biology. Cells vary in size, but typically they are about a micron across, that is, about one ten-thousandth of a centimeter. An active cell divides into two cells about every twenty minutes.

The word *life* itself conjures up animation, movement, excitement, and perhaps a little mystery. Discussions of the origin of life disturb some people. Some are particularly disturbed by scientists who "tamper with creation" and actually try to start life in a laboratory. It would disturb me more to find that life *couldn't* be started in a laboratory. If life can't be started somehow in this physical world, then how did I get here? You see, I *think* I'm alive, although some of you might observe me dozing at my desk and wonder.

The human cell has near its center a nucleus containing forty-six chromosomes. Twenty-three of these come from the father and twenty-three from the mother. The chromosomes are made up of about a million genes that constitute our inheritance. A gene controls the synthesis of essential molecules, such as enzymes, that build and regulate our unbelievably complicated bodies.

A colleague, Frank Johnson, and I once wrote a paper on evolution and rate theory, "The Critical Complex Theory of Biogenesis." This paper outlines a theory of prebiological evolution. One of the principal questions addressed is why living things are optically active.

The body is made up of many types of molecules, just as a large building may be made up of many types of brick. Many of these molecules are asymmetrical, and frequently one optical isomer is found to occur in living things to the virtual exclusion of its mirror image. We can understand this selective choice of building blocks if we recognize that the body is built up by molecules that are to be incorporated into the body from the food we eat. This selection is made by a process of fitting of the molecules to the enzyme much as a left hand selects a left-hand glove and rejects a right-hand glove.

Muscles and enzymes are made by joining amino acids together into long chains called proteins. There are twenty different amino acids that are joined together in different proportions to form the links in the various types of protein chains. Of these twenty amino acids used by the body, all but one are asymmetric. Further, all the nineteen asymmetric amino acids used are like the left-hand glove and are called l-amino acids. In every living thing, the opposite optical isomers, which are called the d-amino acids, if present in the food, are rejected by the enzymes that build proteins, and are eliminated from the body. We therefore call this world we live in an l-amino acid world. The "l" comes from *laevo*, the Latin word for left; and "d" stands for *dextro*, or right.

Using absolute rate theory, Johnson and I arrived at a reasonable rate of appearance of these optically active templates, given assumed concentrations of certain chemicals in the primordial "soup."

The interesting thing is that from any given pot of "soup" it is as likely that a d- as an l-type world will start up. We can readily imagine a d-amino acid world. In fact, if we look into a large mirror, the world we see is a d-amino acid world, since every object, including the molecules, is the mirror image of those in the real world. Obviously, everything in the d-amino acid world would work exactly as well as everything in our real world, and it is a matter of no obvious consequence which world we happen to have. If there are other worlds that support life, there is no reason for supposing that they may not be d-amino acid worlds. If so, such worlds would be completely inhospitable to us, since we could not digest their foods, and marriages between people coming from d and l worlds would necessarily be sterile. On the other hand, there is, of course, no reason why people from two such worlds might not converse with each other with complete understanding, and one could not tell the two types of people apart by their appearance.

The fact that in our world every living thing, from the tiniest living cell to man, uses only the l-amino acids along with the d-sugars highlights the unity running through the living world. Everything that grows collects those particular optical isomers needed for food and rejects the opposite isomers. Here again, we catch a glimpse of the unity that everywhere characterizes the cosmic design.

The fourth world is the world of everyday. Here, we

measure time in seconds or minutes, and distances in feet or miles. This is the world we know most about.

Sir Isaac Newton discovered the universal law of gravitation and developed the laws of mechanics so that his successors have been able to calculate the motion of the planets in their orbits to any desired degree of accuracy. Astronomers predict exactly when an eclipse will occur. Using this knowledge, men make great preparations, assemble expensive scientific equipment, and move to the ends of the earth when told that an eclipse is imminent. They get their cameras ready to take pictures and open the shutters at the right moment, and the eclipse begins at the predicted instant. If the eclipse were ever so little off schedule, it would make headline news around the world.

These same laws that enable astronomers to compute eclipses tell precisely, of course, how a satellite goes around in its orbit. A man who makes a good running broad jump only misses becoming an earth satellite by not running fast enough. Thus, if instead of running twenty miles an hour he ran twenty thousand miles an hour, he would find that as he jumped, the earth would curve away beneath him faster than he could fall toward it. Our jumper would settle into an elliptical orbit extending around the earth, except for one thing—the air resistance would slow his speed and set him on fire. To avoid air resistance, the satellite is shot above the atmosphere. This is the only reason for sending it up six hundred miles.

Satellites like Sputnik and the moon have a terrifically frustrating job. The moon has been falling toward the earth and overshooting the mark for billions of years and still has no prospect for a successful hit. Man has not succeeded in sending satellites up to such complete frustration yet. The reason is simple. Even at altitudes of six hundred or a thousand miles there is still a trace of hydrogen left. As the satellite circles the earth, it bumps into gas. When it has bumped into a weight of gas equal to its mass, its momentum is cut in half, except that by falling closer to the earth it picks up additional speed. Still, it is a remarkable human achievement to launch a satellite and in a small degree become a partner in creation.

All such achievements rely on the fundamental belief that the everyday world is exactly predictable. We may not yet know or completely understand the rules of when earthquakes occur, or what causes surprises for the weatherman, but we are sure that such events are not really capricious. The more we learn, the better we understand and the closer are our predictions.

If we look at the stars, we see the fifth world. Men have probably always looked up and wondered: How far away are the stars? What makes them shine? How long have they been there? Will they exist forever? Some have believed that the stars were gods who controlled their destiny. Others noticed the regularity in the grouping of stars and used their knowledge of stellar movement to help mark the passage of the seasons and fix the times of planting and harvesting. The early Greeks believed the stars were fixed like nails to the vault of the heavens. Aristotle maintained that celestial objects were permanent, immutable, and perfect. He so convinced the Greeks of this that when a new star appeared in 134 B.C. it was attributed by its discoverer to an omission by his predecessors.

In the Middle Ages, Copernicus showed that the earth was not the center of the solar system. But Aristotle's thinking continued to dominate astronomy until the 1500s when new stars were discovered and then in the seventeenth century when Galileo used his telescope to discover spots on the sun—demonstrating that the solar complexion was somewhat less than perfect—and to prove that the sky was filled with stars that could not be seen with the naked eye.

Just so you know how old I am, I can remember when astronomers, using ever-larger telescopes, discovered that some of the "stars" thought to be part of the Milky Way were actually other galaxies—each containing billions of stars and lying far beyond the Milky Way's outermost limits.

Even so today, as we look out at the universe, the first impression is one of stupendous size. By using such instruments as the huge 200-inch optical telescope on Mount Palomar and newer radio, X-ray, and gamma-ray telescopes, modern-day stargazers have pushed the frontiers of understanding ever closer to the edges of the universe and into the very cores of the stars. We can see out so far that the light reaching our eyes started on its journey toward us almost 12 billion years ago. You remember how fast light travels: 186,000 miles a second; it goes around the earth, a distance of 24,000 miles, seven and one-half times in a second. A light-year is the distance that light travels in a year—about 6 trillion miles. If you multiply 12 billion years by 6 trillion miles, you get a seven followed by twenty-two zeros for the number of miles you can see in any direction you care to look. The known radius of the universe in miles is even bigger than the national debt. It is a very long distance indeed.

When you walk outside on a clear moonless night, all the celestial objects you can see with the naked eye are either planets or stars, or, if you have superman vision, you might be able to see the Andromeda galaxy that looks like a fuzzy star. All the stars you see are part of our own Milky Way galaxy. The closest star, other than our own sun, is Proxima Centauri, four light-years away. At our present rates of space travel, this journey would require one hundred twenty thousand years. Consequently, we seem to be marooned in our solar system, at least for the time being. Present missile travel, which proceeds at a speed about a thousand times as fast as man can run, will need to be speeded up by another factor of a thousand before we can undertake trips beyond our solar system.

Some scientists believe that the universe is the expanding remnant of a huge fireball created 20 billion years ago by a giant explosion. The stars and planets are the products of that cataclysmic blast and its aftereffects. In 1929 astronomer Edwin Hubble used shifts in the spectral lines of light coming from distant galaxies to calculate that these islands of stars are moving at tremendous speeds away from the earth—and from each other—like dots painted on the surface of an expanding balloon. Scientists at Bell Laboratories have even listened with their sensitive radio antenna to radiation interference, which amounts to the hissing echoes of creation: "In the beginning God created the heaven and the earth. And the earth was without form, and void; and darkness was upon the face of the deep. And the Spirit of God moved upon the face of the waters. And God said, Let there be light: and there was light." (Genesis 1:1–3.)

Most cosmologists—scientists who study the structure and evolution of the universe—agree that the biblical account of creation, in imagining an initial void, is uncannily close to the truth. I might add, it is as if the one who wrote those words was there, or at least had talked to Someone who was.

Are we the only worshipers in this great cathedral called the universe? Professor Harlow Shapley, emeritus professor of astronomy at Harvard University, has written an interesting book, *Of Stars and Men* (New York: Washington Square Press, Inc., 1960) in which he estimates that there are 100 million, million, million, million suns in space. Shapley has very conservatively estimated that at least one sun in a thousand should have acquired planets. Most of these satellites are at such distances from their suns that they are either too hot or too cold to support life as we know it. Still others lack life-giving water, while others lack the necessary oxygen. However, Shapley has estimated that of those suns with planets at least one in a thousand has a planet at the right distance for life.

Of those having a planet at the right distance, at least

one in a thousand should have a planet large enough to hold an atmosphere, and, finally, that one in a thousand of those having a large enough planet at the right distance should have an atmosphere of the right composition to support life. Thus, he concludes that there should be at the very minimum 100 million planets that could support life, and the number is probably many times more. From the scientific point of view, it is hard to doubt that myriads of worlds are suitable for human habitation.

It is accordingly natural to conclude that the universe is filled with intelligent beings and, presumably, always has been. Any unfolding of intelligences on this earth only repeats what has happened previously elsewhere. Even if we believe beings on distant planets have progressed far beyond us, still the barrier to travel posed by interstellar distances seems quite sufficient to explain why mortal space travelers have not visited us.

So we envision a still-expanding universe that began almost 20 billion years ago, extends for 12 billion light-years, and contains 10 billion galaxies—each one an island of hundreds of billions of stars. Actually, we also need to add the dimension of time. We see our nearby sun as it looked a little more than eight minutes ago. We see Proxima Centauri as it was about four years ago, and some of the farther galaxies as they looked billions of years ago. The farther out we look, the further we are looking back in time. Some objects we see may no longer exist.

With all that we do know, it is obvious to the serious student that there is a great deal more that we don't know. To the ultimate question—what existed before the big bang—most of modern science is mute. It's as if it were against the rules to ask questions when there isn't any scientific way to approach the answers. It's still a nice question though, isn't it?

From nucleus to galaxies, the universe is complex, orderly, consistent, and very, very interesting. It is also full of energy and motion. There is something peculiar about that.

If you picked up a watch far from human habitation and found it running, you would ask not only "Who made this watch?" but "Who wound it up?" So it is with the universe. The universe is running down. It is a universe of change. People are born and pass from the earth, and stars, too, come into existence and pass away.

The sun is about half hydrogen; the rest of it is composed of other materials. The hydrogen bomb shows us what happens to hydrogen down in the center of the sun where the pressures and temperatures are enormous. Four hydrogen atoms come together to make helium, and, in the process, a little of their weight is changed into energy. This energy falls on the earth as sunlight and makes the plants grow.

Thus, the sun is a giant furnace with a supply of hydrogen for fuel—quite a good supply. But if the sun ever burns out, it is going to be very cold in Salt Lake City. You might like an estimate of the fuel supply on hand. I would say the supply should last at least five billion years, so we don't need to worry about it right away.

This picture of the sun as a furnace with a limited amount of fuel poses interesting problems. The second law of thermodynamics is a formal statement of the familiar fact that if energy is being obtained continuously from some source, then the supply of energy must run out sometime unless it is replenished from an outside source. As with any woodpile, if you keep burning up the hydrogen on the sun, it must ultimately be used up unless it is replenished. There is evidence that in the last billion years the sun's temperature has never varied by the small amount that would make the earth unfit for habitation.

It is a well-known fact of experience that if we set a pot of boiling water on a table in a cool room, the pot cools, and when once cooled it never returns to the boiling point without being reheated. In just the same way the sun is giving off its heat and very gradually growing colder. When the sun ceases to shine, all living things will die; all changes will cease, and the world will reach a deadly, monotonous uniformity. This state is called the *heat death* and is a consequence of nature always moving toward more probable states and never in the reverse direction toward less probable states.

An interesting calculation illustrates the complete improbability of a hot sun arising by chance. We suppose that in order to become hot again the sun must accumulate an amount of heat equal to that it gives off during its lifetime. This must be accumulated from its surroundings, which we shall assume in the heat death drops to a temperature of 700 degrees centigrade. Then, using the straightforward theory of chemical reactions, we find that a length of time in years equal to at least one with a hundred thousand, billion, billion, billion, billion, billion zeros must elapse before a hot sun has a 50-percent probability of occurring again by chance. This is almost no chance at all! A universe *filled* with hot suns is no more likely. It is evident that our hot sun, or this universe, did not arise by such a chance fluctuation.

In a very real sense, then, the universe is like a clock that has been wound up. If it is self-winding, it is unique in scientific experience. In a talk before the National Academy of Sciences, I raised the obvious question, "How did the universe get wound up?" No one chose to answer. After the talk, I repeated my question privately to three scientists. President Millikan of the California Institute of Technology said, "I, like you, am a religious man." Professor Van Vleck of the Harvard physics department said, "Of course, one doesn't know." The third man said, "Don't you believe in your religion?" I answered, "Yes, but I wondered about yours."

# THE SPIRITUAL WORLD

The five physical worlds display order and complexity. The second law of thermodynamics tells us that, even if we can explain this complexity, we have a problem of how it all got started within the working of the natural laws as we understand them. This leaves scientists no better off than anyone else. We *all* have to rely on a very small measure of information and a very large measure of faith.

This brings us, then, to the sixth world, which includes and surrounds all the others. This is the world that existed before the "big bang." It is the world of the Creator, who provided the energy to wind up the watch and the knowledge and power to establish the complex order we have come to understand in the five physical worlds. As far as we know, this sixth world is without beginning and end of space and of time. Presiding over all is the Creator, whom we worship. Holding everything together are the eternal laws, which will require an eternity for us to master.

One of the first Soviet cosmonauts who circled the earth in space boasted on his return that he hadn't seen anything of God on his journey. This raises the interesting question of where the sixth world and its inhabitants are. Is heaven part of the physical universe as we know it, or is it in some other time and space—in another dimension?

Let's consider the notion of postulates. Postulates are those fundamental propositions that are assumed without proof, generally because there is no way to prove them other than to see if the theories built on them predict events that are then verified by experiments. For example, we all learned as part of our high-school geometry class the postulate that parallel lines never meet. This is a postulate of euclidian geometry. However, if you are willing to walk far enough, I can show you a problem. If you and a friend both start out at the equator and walk due north, you are walking parallel paths. You both start out at right angles to the equator. But, you will meet at the North Pole! (You can check this out by looking at two different degrees of longitude on a globe. Each intersects the equator at a 90-degree angle, but they meet at the poles.) The problem is that plane geometry works only on a plane, a flat, two-dimensional world. It doesn't work when the plane curves into a third dimension.

This points up the importance of examining our postulates, our assumptions. Whether or not a particular theory actually predicts reality or not is more a function of the underlying assumptions than of the elegance of the proof itself. Thus, euclidian geometry is perfect for the flat world for which it was designed, but it results in poor predictions in a three-dimensional world.

The same kind of problem occurs when we begin considering the sixth world. If it curves into a fourth or tenth or hundredth dimension, what basic assumptions should we adopt? Can nothing there travel faster than the speed of light, as in our world? What kind of matter are things made of? Are they subject to the pull of gravity? When they bump against our matter does it hurt? Or do they pass right through? How can we find out?

The avenue to religious faith lies in the examination of evidence. The Lord himself outlined the procedure when he said, "If any man will do his will, he shall know of the doctrine, whether it be of God, or whether I speak of myself." (John 7:17.)

The existence of the sixth world is necessary to an understanding of the other five. Put another way, the existence of the five worlds can be adequately explained only if we assume the existence of the sixth world. Of course, we can also look for evidence of the sixth world in history, and directly, by exercising that part of us that shares that other, spiritual dimension.

I worship the wisest being in the universe. I know there is a wisest being in the universe because you can take the wisest person in a room and say, "This is the smartest man in the room—and his wife is smarter." And then you can find the smartest person in the city, then state, then country, then world, then universe. I worship the wisest being in the universe. I know there is such a being. How could there not be? People are different in understanding, and there are lots of them. There must be one who is the smartest.

So I know there is a God. You say, "That still isn't religion." I say, "It is to me, because I can't believe that this wisest being in the universe wants anything except justice." You see, I know some things about him. If you went out in your car tonight and were hit by a drunk driver and killed, there are others who would say, "Isn't it a tragedy that he couldn't live out his life, that he was cut off?" And do you know what they would do if they could? They'd give you another chance.

The wisest being in the universe is surely as compassionate as these good neighbors that we have. He must like justice and not injustice. So I know there is a God. Because otherwise the world would be unjust. This idea takes us a long way toward understanding God. He exists. He is compassionate. He loves justice and relates to us. We are his children. Isn't that a comforting thought? I'm sure of it, but you don't want to believe anything I say unless it's true.

I can say that I am certain that God is just as real as anybody I know, and that he likes me. And that he likes you too. Those are my postulates for the sixth, spiritual world. They perform exactly the same function in helping me understand the sixth world as the postulates of science do in helping me understand the other five.

# DUALITY IN NATURE AND GOD

Sir Isaac Newton, three hundred years ago, thought of light moving in straight lines and in general behaving much as material particles would. This point of view was given up when the Dutchman Huygens showed that many experiments involving light could be better understood if we thought of light as waves being deflected much as water waves are deflected by the obstructions on a pond. Still later, Maxwell developed the general theory of the wave nature of light to such a degree of perfection that the particle theory seemed completely discredited. The interesting point is that everyone felt that the particle theory and the wave theory of light were mutually exclusive. Light could be a particle or a wave, but it could not be both.

Then, in 1905, Albert Einstein published his theory of the photoelectric effect, for which he was given the Nobel Prize. If light hits a metal surface, electrons are ejected, provided the light is violet enough. Further, the energy with which the electron is ejected is proportional to the frequency of the light and to nothing else. This can be understood if light is made up of particles with energy proportional to their frequency. Einstein called these light particles *photons*, and with the acceptance of this particle theory, a full-blown paradox was born.

Physicists were at first thoroughly disturbed by this split

personality exhibited by light, but as time went on they learned to live with it. It is now accepted that light is made up of the particle-like photons which, however, are accompanied by a wave that governs the direction in which light travels. On the other hand, whenever photons are absorbed by matter, they are swallowed up as a unit, just as any other particle might be.

In the middle 1920s, DeBroglie predicted that particles of matter would be found to have waves associated with them controlling their direction of travel just as light particles have. When a beam of electrons all having the same velocity is directed against a crystal, it is deflected just as light is. Accordingly, we must also think of matter as showing schizophrenic behavior, sometimes acting like a wave and sometimes like a particle. Again, physicists have learned to live with the unexpected behavior.

If we read the story of Robert E. Lee, the great military tactician, we find that even at a large battlefield as complex as Gettysburg, his army was maneuvered as though Lee himself were storming Cemetery Ridge alongside Pickett, as well as being everywhere else on the battlefield. Lee's success as a general depended to a very great extent on the gathering of information about the strength, position, and intentions of his adversary both before and during the battle. The result is that any story of Lee as a general would tell about his influence permeating the whole sphere of his activities and very little about Lee the man. In this sense Lee is two people, the man, like anyone else, and the far-flung intelligence system that governed the motion of him and his army much as a wave is spread out in space and governs the motion of a photon or a material particle.

In an analogous manner, we may think of God as the all-wise arbiter of the universe, with his infinite wisdom having an influence that permeates the most remote recesses of space, and yet being himself an exalted being with personality and deep concern for struggling humanity.

The strange thing is that many people have a struggle with this concept of God having a dual nature. On the one hand are those who prefer God to have only a wave nature—a Universal Mind providing order to the universe, everywhere present but not tied down to any locality. They may reject the idea of a kind of Heavenly Father who loves and cares about us, his children, as being a wishful fairytale.

On the other hand are those who emphasize the particle nature and may fail to understand how much different God is from man. That is, they focus on the similarities—"As man is God once was; as God is man may become" or "God created man in his own image" and miss the enormous differences. It is God who orchestrated the "big bang" 20 billion years ago and set the universe on its way. He it is who devised, promulgated, and now enforces the laws of nature with never-failing accuracy and consistency. I think we may have been with him in the beginning and, as his children, may have participated in some small way. I also believe that we have the opportunity of progressing and eventually coming to be like him, but I have no illusions about how far we have to go. It is a very long way.

One interesting observation I might make has to do with Einstein's religious views. He always said that Spinoza, the philosopher, who had converted in Holland from Judaism to Christianity, was his idea of the most important religious leader. Spinoza believed that God ruled the universe, but that God was very far away. Philosophers would call Spinoza a deist. Mormons would be called theists. We believe that when we pray to God, he hears and influences human affairs. Einstein didn't think that that happened, but he did believe, and used his belief in getting his general theory of relativity, that God wouldn't play tricks. So Einstein assumed that when he knew one law, he could guess another. He said something to the effect that the difficult thing to understand about the universe is that it is understandable. So, I'd have to classify him as a religious man. He was born a Jew but was not interested in Judaism. I don't think he went to synagogue very often, if ever.

Anyway, I find it interesting that Einstein, who won the Nobel Prize for demonstrating that light has both a particle and wave nature, might not have understood or believed that God is both a personage with body and location and a power and influence pervading everything, everywhere. (See D&C 88:41.)

# COMMUNICATION

Communicating is one of the most important things we do. We are in this world together, and what a lonesome place it would be if we were really alone. Can you imagine anything worse than Robinson Crusoe without Friday? That would be about the saddest thing we could have. It emphasizes to me the importance of working together.

Communication of information involves both a sender and a receiver. The gospel flows from the Creator of the world who sees the end from the beginning. It flows to all who are able to receive it. Too many of those who are blind and deaf to this flow of information foolishly deny the existence of the Creator.

Written in the many languages of the world are all sorts of messages that completely escape us because we don't speak those particular languages. We haven't yet found the appropriate Rosetta stone.

Soon after my family first arrived in Pima, Arizona, our horses got loose one night and broke into Bishop Philemon Merrill's alfalfa fields next door. Those horses felt awfully good the next morning when I was given the chore of getting them out. Just as I was about to coax the last horse through the gate, the whole herd broke and ran back into the fields, and I had to start all over again. When they broke for the second time, all my patience was gone, and I began explaining the situation to them in very descriptive terms.

It was a performance I'm still ashamed of. I was finally able to get them out, but I had been overheard by Charles Ferron, who had the farm on the other side of Bishop Merrill's place.

Three years later I went to work for Brother Ferron for several summers, which helped our family finances considerably. On one occasion he asked me, "Henry, do you know the first time I ever saw you?" I said, "No, I don't know." He said, "Do you remember when you were getting horses out of Bishop Merrill's?" I acknowledged uneasily that I did. He said, "I'll tell you what I said—I said, 'It would have been all right if Brother Eyring had just drowned that boy when he was born.'" I think by then I had redeemed myself with Brother Ferron, but it was an uphill struggle. What I needed was a better way to communicate with those confounded horses.

Anyway, communications are essential to our functioning in the world and to our relationship with its Creator. The Creator of the universe has implanted a message in every created thing. Geology, astronomy, physics—all science is really nothing more than an effort to read those messages.

The universe is so large that the best reflecting telescopes enable us to see stars by light that started journeying toward us 12 billion years ago. The subsequent history of these stars is completely unknown. They may have long since ceased to exist. Do you think the Lord ever goes out there? If he does, when you pray to him out there what happens? Nobody on earth knows how to send a message faster than the velocity of light. And so, if you prayed today and the Lord was on the far side of his ranch, clear out there at the farthest star, it would take 12 billion years for your prayer to get there and another 12 billion years for an answer to get back. By that time, it would be out of date.

I don't really know the solution to this hypothetical problem, but that doesn't keep me from telling you what I believe. I think either the Lord has an organization that takes care of things or else he has a way of communicating (which I suspect is true) very much faster than anything we know about. In fact, there seems no reasonable alternative to the conclusion that the Creator has methods of immediate communication unknown and perhaps unknowable to man.

Somehow, the universe is coordinated and regulated by influences that transcend the laws of physics now known. I don't think that just because people on this planet don't know how to send messages any faster is any proof to me that God doesn't know how to do it. So I'm going to pray just the same, no matter whether he's all the way at the other side of the ranch or just part way. He's running this thing. I know that because of how magnificently it runs.

# REVELATION AND MIRACLES

One of the great messages of the gospel is that there is such a thing as revelation. After I had been at the University of Utah for three or four years, one of the regents of the university, a fine lady, not a member of the Church, said, "Dr. Eyring, I can understand how you as a scientist are religious, but I can't understand how you could believe in a *revealed* religion." But if I believe in a God who cares about us and is capable of doing anything, how can I *not* believe in revelation? I can't believe in a religion that doesn't accept that whenever it suits the Lord's purpose, he reveals things to us. That is the great message that the Prophet Joseph Smith brought back to the world.

Now I think there are plenty of times when God probably doesn't think it necessary to get involved. For instance, I've been asked whether I think God helps me with my science. That is, does God steer human efforts such as scientific study? I don't think God cares very much about reaction rate theory. He's known it all along. All he does is in his mind reach out his hand and pat me on the head and say, "That's a nice little fellow. It's nice that you try." I think he cares about how I treat my fellowmen and is not very much impressed with the rest. On his scale, as Creator of the universe, what I have done couldn't be very impressive. After all, he can do integral calculus in his head.

In a long life, I have seen a number of things that border on the miraculous and, to my mind, indicate divine intervention. I recently visited with a dear friend almost my own age who at the age of three was gored by a wild cow. About a yard of his intestines was strewn out on the ground, ruptured in several places. A country doctor was called from town about eight miles away. After arriving in his buggy, he washed the intestines with water as best he could and sewed up the ruptures. He then pushed the intestines back through the hole they had come out of and sewed up the hole in the belly. The doctor went back to town and waited for the family to come make funeral arrangements.

Infection set in, as was inevitable. The family, however, were devout, and they and their friends anointed and blessed the small boy and asked the Lord to spare him. After a few days when no one came to town, the doctor drove out to the ranch to see what had happened. He found the small boy sitting up. The lad's question startled the doctor. It was, "What have you brought me today?" The doctor remarked, "Some power far beyond mine is at work here." Experiences such as this could be multiplied almost indefinitely. Just a natural occurrence? Perhaps, but I don't think so.

The stirring story of Paul on the road to Damascus and the experience that changed him from an implacable foe of the Saints to their foremost defender is as compelling now as it was when it happened. No explanation of these events is as satisfying to me as Paul's own interpretation. He gladly dedicated his life to proclaiming the gospel, and at the end went unflinching to a martyr's death. Was he mistaken? I believe not.

Joseph Smith's story is strikingly similar. His experiences in the Sacred Grove and in many places afterward removed all doubt from his mind. For him, also, a life of dedication led to a martyr's grave. Was he wrong? I don't think so.

Now, what about the miracles of the Bible? Did Moses really turn the Nile to blood, or part the Red Sea? Did manna fall from heaven? First of all, the topic is hardly worth talking about. I don't know the answer, and it doesn't make any difference anyway. These are historical events and can't be confirmed by laboratory experimentation, but if someone could prove to me *conclusively* that any such miracle in the Bible didn't really happen, but was just hyperbole on the part of the writer or some later translator, I wouldn't lose my testimony. After all, I'm only interested in finding out what the truth is. The only miracle I can think of that makes a difference is the resurrection of Jesus Christ. Whether or not manna really fell from heaven or was just the dried sap of the tamarisk plants in the area doesn't seem to me to have much religious significance.

Second, the Creator of the universe almost certainly knows enough about how things work to control and manipulate events to meet his purposes, either within the rules of natural law or outside them, if necessary. Now, as a scientist, I'm not very enthusiastic about the notion of shoving natural laws aside. I prefer to keep things orderly and predictable. But, as we've noted already, I suspect the Lord can send messages faster than the speed of light, and so, even if natural law, as we understand it, had to be suspended in order for the Savior to walk on the Sea of Galilee, I certainly don't see even that as being an insurmountable problem for the Creator of the universe.

In summary, I accept Jesus as the Son of God, whether or not he walked on the water, and I can't see any reason why he, as the Creator of this world, wouldn't have the power to do it if he wanted to. Revelations and miracles seem like the natural consequences of having a compassionate and just Creator of the universe interested in human events.

# BEFORE LIFE, AND AFTER

While I was at Princeton, on one occasion Einstein came to a lecture at the University. It was raining, and Dr. Hugh Taylor suggested that we give Einstein a ride home. I don't remember how it came up. Maybe I asked him the Golden Questions. In any case, on the way home I told him that we as Mormons believe in a premortal existence. Not only do we believe in a life after death, but that we lived before we came here. He asked, "What about dogs?" I told him I was a little weak on dogs, but that since we believe that all things are created spiritually before they are created temporally, that God would take care of dogs, too. He seemed to be awfully relieved about that, but he was not so impressed that he immediately asked for baptism. He was very courteous and gracious, however.

Have we lived before? Will we live again? These questions must be almost as old as thought itself. The poet William Wordsworth, in "Ode: Intimations of Immortality from Recollections of Early Childhood," voiced this unforgettable thought in this way:

*Our birth is but a sleep and a forgetting:*
*The Soul that rises with us, our life's Star,*
*Hath had elsewhere its setting,*
*And cometh from afar:*
*Not in entire forgetfulness,*

*And not in utter nakedness,*
*But trailing clouds of glory do we come*
*From God, who is our home.*

To accept the idea that the human personality ends with death is to accept life as a futile, meaningless gesture. Every one of us has friends and loved ones who, if they had the knowledge and power, would preserve us and keep us as companions forever. God has that knowledge and power. He would be less compassionate than many good men if life ended at the grave.

Broken, uncompleted lives are the best possible reason for a hereafter in which the scales of justice are balanced by a just God. To believe otherwise is to attribute to God a lack of sensitivity that we find regularly in good men. Such a supposition is incredible to me. One sees good people cut off by death in their prime. It is impossible to reconcile such incompleteness with any other idea than that we will live again and that what we have lost through no fault of our own will be made up to us in full by a just God. Erwin Schrödinger, the scientist responsible for initiating wave mechanics, was convinced that nothing as remarkable as the human spirit could dissolve into nothingness.

To believe in the immortality of individuals is necessarily to believe in God, since the perpetuation of personality beyond this life without divine interposition is difficult to imagine. Also, if we consider the immense complexity of our mortal body, which works, it is easy to trust the Creator to supply a suitable tabernacle for the next stage of the journey.

We certainly don't know how the resurrection will take place nor how closely the immortal body will be a copy of our mortal one. However, we have learned some very interesting things about regeneration. Just as a salamander can regenerate a limb if it is cut off, so a single human cell, with its chromosomes, has in it the blueprints for generating the whole human body. A knowledge of the responsible molecular blueprints, the chromosomes, and of how to nurture the resultant cell would make it possible to completely regenerate the body, perhaps out of better materials. We also know that at inception life begins as a single cell that carries within it all the blueprints for fashioning the mature body. Further, simply recounting to us the events of earth life would restore to us our past. No doubt this is not the way immortality will be ushered in, but it should suffice to show that even we simple mortals can see the possibility of immortality. How much simpler it must seem to the Creator.

Just what God has in store for us is another puzzle. He's revealed to us some rules for life and at least a broad sketch of what is to come. If we have sense enough to listen, we've got it made. If we don't, it will take a little longer. He's not going to give up on us, if he can help it. He may have to place some of us honorable men of the world in the terrestrial kingdom and some of us, who just insist on being naughty, he may place in the telestial kingdom.

I have a vivid, if inaccurate, image of hell. After I got a master's degree in metallurgy, I went to work in Clarkdale, Arizona, at the United Verde smelter. As a prospective metallurgist, I was taking samples out of the twenty blast furnaces. The superintendent came up to me, slapped me on the shoulder, and said, "Eyring, I like the way you're working out. If you stay here a few weeks I'm going to put you in charge of all twenty blast furnaces." Well, you should have seen the sulfur smoke coming out of there. It looked like the devil himself was running the place. I put a handkerchief dipped in bicarbonate over my face just so I could breathe. I can tell you, when the opportunity came I didn't have any trouble taking a teaching job back at the University of Arizona. I figured that if I misbehaved, I wouldn't be any worse off in the hereafter than working in that smelter.

Now they say that the telestial kingdom really isn't that bad, but I wouldn't try for it. I'm counting on going to the best, which you're not supposed to say, but at least let's have our sights high. I hope the Lord will say, "That man Eyring is not too hot. He could have been lots better. But he also could have been a lot worse. Let's have him in here to smile at." I hope he'll also say, "His good wives would like to have him with them, so let's let him in." So I'm planning on going, but to make it as sure as possible, I'm also working at it as hard as I can.

# SCIENCE AND RELIGION

God likes me and won't give up on me no matter what. He'll keep encouraging and praising me when he can, chastise when he must, but never stop hoping that I'll make something out of myself. He is so much more advanced than I am he couldn't be very impressed with my wisdom; it's my effort that really counts. I'm not apt to teach him anything he hasn't already known for a long time. One of the nicest things is his tolerance of us.

Once when I was speaking at the University of Utah as part of a panel on man in the cosmos, I built my talk around the famous question of Pontius Pilate, "What is truth?" After my talk, a young man in the audience stood up and said, "Well, Dr. Eyring, they tell me that what you do is put religion in one compartment and your science in another. Isn't that inconvenient? For instance, I want to propound a question to you. In the *Young Women's Journal*, Joseph Smith is reported to have said that people are living on the moon." He continued, "Now, Dr. Eyring, we know there is no oxygen on the moon, so that couldn't possibly be true. What do you say to this question?"

I answered about as follows: "I especially appreciate being asked that question, because it is easy to answer, and I like easy questions better than hard ones. As a Latter-day Saint, like any other honest man, I am obliged to accept only the truth. I simply have to investigate whether men live on the moon. I am reasonably certain they don't, but we'll soon know by direct exploration. If we don't find them there, they don't live there. As a Latter-day Saint, my problem is as simple as that.

"Many times men of importance have statements attributed to them they never made. I think that if J. Golden Kimball said all the things he is credited with saying, he would have had to talk even more than he did, and he did very well.

"Now what about the Prophet Joseph Smith? I don't know whether or not he said men live on the moon. But whether he did or not troubles me not in the least. A prophet is wonderful because he sometimes speaks for the Lord. This occurs on certain occasions when the Lord wills it. On other occasions, he speaks for himself, and one of the wonderful doctrines of this Church is that we don't believe in the infallibility of any mortal. If in his speculations the Prophet thought there were people on the moon, this has no effect on my belief that on other occasions, when the Lord willed it, he spoke the ideas that the Lord inspired him to say. It is for these moments of penetrating insight that I honor and follow him."

There is a further point that needs emphasis. The gospel is not the people in the Church. The gospel is not even the people who direct it. *The gospel is the truth*. One will have difficulty finding better men than we have presiding over the Church at present and than we have had in times past. Still, they are human beings, as we are.

Some people have pointed to some member of the Church and said, "Now, Dr. Eyring, that's one of your brethren, and he's not what he ought to be." My answer is this: "Well, you ought to see what he'd be like if it weren't for the Church." We have to keep firmly in mind at all times the two aspects of the Church: its divinely inspired perfect side, and its human side.

Perhaps I can say it another way. This Church would have been perfect if the Lord had not let people into it.

That is where the mistake seems to have been made, but we understand this, too. The Church is part of the Lord's wonderful plan to work with you and me. Mankind is thus singled out because of man's divine origin and transcendent destiny.

I could leave the Church and abandon its teachings if I could figure out some way to do so honorably and consistent with my desire to know the truth, no matter what the source. I find myself unable to build out of my experience an acceptable case for disbelief. In fact, the case favors belief. It goes something like this:

1. The physical universe exhibits striking characteristics: the complexity of the nucleus, the exactness of the atom, the unity of life, the predictability of the everyday world, and the enormity and longevity of space.

2. Not only is the universe complex, exact, orderly, and predictable, but it is also running down. The second law of thermodynamics indicates that since a closed system can only run down and can never get wound up in the first place, either there are some exceptions to these natural laws we don't know about or the physical universe is not a closed system. That is, there is something or someplace outside the physical world from which energy was obtained to fire the "big bang."

3. The combination of intelligence and power that assembled the materials and energy, set off the "big bang," and provided order, complexity, exactness, and precision in the physical universe is called the Creator, the Supreme Being, God, and so on.

4. As scientists believe that nature is not capricious, and therefore we can expect things we can't measure to behave in ways similar to things we can, it is reasonable to assume that the Creator's world is also a place of order, complexity, exactness, and precision. This is an example of the importance of postulates in science and religion. In order to seek to learn truths about the physical world we must *assume*

some things we can't prove. (An example is uniformitarianism—the proposition that the rules as we now observe them were the same in the past and will be in the future and that therefore we can understand the past and predict the future based on what we observe now.) Similarly, in order to seek for truth in spiritual things, we must adopt some basic assumptions or postulates that also can't be proved.

5. Basic spiritual assumptions or postulates might include: (a) God exists; (b) God has curiosity and interest in what he has created; (c) God knows me; (d) God is at least as compassionate and just as the good people I know.

6. The truth of these postulates is determined by seeing if the results of "experiments" can be best predicted by their adoption. That is, as we experience life, study history, and seek communion with God, is what we find best explained by the acceptance of our postulates?

7. God is tolerant of our efforts. He's willing to have truth discovered "line upon line, precept upon precept." That is, he doesn't mind that we don't yet know everything about science, or religion.

8. The gospel is the truth. All truth is part of the gospel regardless of how the truth has been learned.

9. The safest course is to work like the dickens and do even more than is required to be done. That's the way I get the most freedom to maneuver.

10. Most important, the foregoing nine points don't answer *all* the questions. If I take everything I know from the scriptures and the prophets, and everything I know from science, and reconcile them, I still have as many unanswered questions as I have ones with answers. No intellectual approach nails down everything. In this life, there will always be unanswered questions. In fact, each answer seems to raise more questions. That's the way it is in science, too, and I don't apostatize from science for that reason. Actually, that's what makes science, and religion, fun. Faith is feeling

good about myself, feeling good about God, and muddling along after truth as best I can.

11. Finally, perhaps a believer never does more disservice to religion than to support the truth with bad arguments. The listener spots the obvious errors, becomes impatient, often "throws out the baby with the bath," and turns away, even from true religion.

As parents and teachers, we pass on to our children and pupils our world picture. Part of this picture is religious and part of it deals with the world around us. If we teach our pupils some outmoded and nonessential notions that fail to hold water when the students get into their science classes at the university, we run grave risks. When our protégés shed the bad science, they may also throw out some true religion. The solution is to avoid telling them the world is flat too long after it has been proved round. Don't defend a good cause with bad arguments.

So, I am certain that the gospel, as taught in The Church of Jesus Christ of Latter-day Saints, is true. It's a better explanation of what I observe in science than any other I know about. There are still lots of things I don't know, but that doesn't bother me. I'm a happy muddler. The gospel simply asks me to find out what's true as best I can and in the meantime to live a good life. That strikes me as the best formula for living there could be.